FRANK SCHNEIDER

GAWD, I LOVE NEW ORLEANS

FLAPS Publisher
6127 Louis XIV St.
New Orleans, LA 70124
504- 486-1824

Graphic design by Escudier & Richard, Inc., New Orleans

This book is a memorial to my darling wife
JOYCE 'HAPPY' PARKS SCHNEIDER

Cover and illustrations by our grandson
CHRISTOPHER ERIC STEGER

References:

Frenchmen, Desire, Good Children by John Chase; Creole Collage by Leonard V. Huber; Standard History of New Orleans edited by Henry Rightor; Gumbo Ya-Ya by Lyle Saxon, Edward Dryer, Robert Tallant; Old New Orleans by Stanley Clisby Arthur; The Times-Picayune New Orleans Guide; The French Quarter by Herbert Asbury; Historic City Park by Sally K. Reeves and William D. Reeves with Ellis Laborde and James S. Janssen; Chronicle of America, Chronicle Publications; The World From Jackson Square edited by Etolia S. Basso; Hurricane by Marjorie Stoneman Douglas, Louisiana the Pelican State by Edwin Adams Davis, and Building New Orleans by James S. Janssen.

Merci beaucoup:

To my dear children whose nagging ("Do it for us, Pop-Pop") stirred me to purchase a computer, ergonomically correct desk and chair. To my son-in-law Keith R. Steger, and Betsy Martinez, Shirley Ann Grau, Donald W. Conway, J. Burdge Walton, Charles R. Brennan, Mary Ellen George, Clare Guilbault, Mary Lou Widmer for their support and professional opinions.

The Tales:

Foreword

Frank Schneider and I have been friends for many decades, and mutual friends will agree with my assessment that he is, above all, a consummate story teller. At a party, he regales his friends with witty stories delivered with the brevity and timing of a standup comic. In his column "Second Cup" he gave his morning readers a good chuckle with his delightful anecdotes and tales of Old New Orleans.

At last, he has captured in a book many facts, legends and personal memories of New Orleans when the twentieth century was new and the city was an overgrown country town.

He reminds us of jambalaya lumpy with sausage and shrimp. He recalls the ladies scrubbing the stoop with Octagon soap, and bargaining with a vendor in a wagon pulled by a horse called Dolly. He recalls Papa sending the oldest boy to "fill-a-pitcha" with beer, and "dunking French bread knots in *cafe au lait*" with his cousin Joyce.

We go with him in memory of the days when clients of Miss Zodarinos' School of the Dance and Acrobatics performed on the stage by the Big Casino in City Park, when nuns at Holy Rosary School fed the stove chunks of wood, and when coffee was dripped in the big white agate pot.

We are carried back in time to the swivel stools in K&B where we ordered chicken salad sandwiches. We recall with him the nine cent bread, the Jumbo drink, knickers, cisterns, spring tonic and a picture of Dad sitting on the car's running board.

In typical New Orleans jargon, he spells out such rib ticklers as Frydy & Saddy, Voo Caw-ray, What-cha-sed and nootroo groun.

If Frank Schneider can say, "Gawd, I love New Orleans," then I can add, "Them's my sentiments."

Mary Lou Widmer

Author's Preface

Please don't read this book as a narrative. It is not intended to be one. It does have a beginning and it has an end, but it is not a story related in sequence. It is simply a personal reflection on life in New Orleans, the small town that passes itself off as a big city.

It relates a bit of history, some facts, folklore, mystique, nostalgia. It includes swatches of those things that make New Orleans beloved by its citizens and stimulate curiosity. There are tales of New Orleans' claims to fame and shame, and its celebrations that keep it ever young and vital.

Each generation has its own appreciation of this spirited city that will go on forever to offer bits of heaven on earth to those who know how to relax in its soothing atmosphere.

This old city's lure is as big as its swamps used to be, and it offers a pleasant stay for all generations - yesterday's, today's, tomorrow's, and to both young and old. If they're not too serious.

BIENVILLE FOUND MY NEIGHBORHOOD, THEN THE CITY ... so to speak

When my favorite explorer and his band of valiant bruisers were on their way to create *Nouvelle Orleans* they ventured into a spongy wilderness. There, Jean Baptiste LeMoyne, Sieur de Bienville, spent a night in my old neighborhood before he found the city.

His consuming ambition to colonize the New World with Frenchmen had begun 19 years earlier when he and his brother Pierre Le Moyne, Sieur de Iberville, searched for a site in the vast territory claimed by Robert Cavelier, Sieur de LaSalle. LaSalle named the land *Louisiane* (Land of Louis) for "Louis le Grand", 14th of France's monarchs to bear the name. For years the brothers pleaded with the king to make the colonial investment. Not until after Iberville's death did Louis agree to finance a town in *Louisiane*.

A happy Bienville sailed from France in 1718 with a fleet of six ships supplied with convicts and other provisions to establish a colony. At Fort Biloxi the adventurers boarded smaller craft and barges, picked up a few Indian guides, and sailed farther west. They came upon a big lake the brothers earlier had named Pontchartrain for France's Marine Minister. Beyond the lake would be the bayou Bienville named for his patron, St. Jean. Along that bayou they would find an ancient footpath, an easy back door approach to a long and tortuous river Indians called *miss ippi,* great water.

Before reaching that footpath Bienville might have waved a mosquito from his nose as he gazed intently at a soggy cypress kingdom surrounding the bayou. The visionary must have fantasized how one day corn would grow and cows would graze there. Indeed, long after cows and corn ventured farther out I would grow up in that scrubby "back of town" spot.

It was a pleasant April day when Bienville's party came

to the bayou three blocks from where my family and Sammy the spitz would reside 213 years later. At one point he faced a wildwood that would become the Creoles' grand Downtown thoroughfare, the 3 1/2 mile *Promenade Publique* (later Esplanade Avenue) from the Mississippi River to the bayou. There, the explorer was 200 or so feet from where my family members would rest in St. Louis Cemetery No. 3 on the avenue, across from where a fading Creole cottage would be my schoolhouse. Behind him would be City Park, my boyhood stomping ground.

Our teachers never once mentioned any of this.

The party continued for a few hundred feet beyond a crook in the bayou when the guides shouted and pointed to the footpath ahead. The weary explorer commanded: "*Nous allons faire du camping*", or something like that.

After camping one night in my old neighborhood, Bienville's team trudged on hauling equipment along the woodsy path (Bayou Road) toward the river. At trail's end men hacked out a clearance for the town's initial neighborhood close to the lapping river water. It became the Vieux Carre (Old Square), a lusty, gutsy colony that would attract aristocrats, peasants, clergy, deadly mosquitoes and, too frequently, the river itself.

From such an embryo was hatched a city a songwriter would call "heaven on earth." Unabashedly, the town was named for the prince regent of France Louis Phillipe duc d'Orleans, premier debaucher of his day. In spite of its bursts of religious fervor, some might say the town was suitably baptized.

Varmints & Storms

Much of the early city was soppy with river water and surrounded by swamplands and cypress woodlands that were inhabited by alligators and other varmints. Because early residents spent lifetimes combating winds, floods, fires and diseases development of my neighborhood was long coming.

Meanwhile, the town grew Downtown, Uptown and across the river remarkably fast. In spite of raging fires, murderous pestilence, and political intrigue growth expanded first to *faubourgs* (suburbs) and *banlieues* (borderlands). Eventually, it spread to "back of town" where Bienville had visited so many springtimes before.

Many Tongues

Resolute planners, engineers and a bullheaded populace turned swamps into firm, green neighborhoods of distinctive character where enterprising residents of varied cultures raised families. With the invasion of Americans the fusion of a half dozen or so tongues left offspring with peculiar speech evident today. The peculiar sounds are referred to as quaint. Perhaps the lumping of humankind in that initial Old Square explains not only a perplexing dialect but a cosmopolis that thrives on its own cuisine, customs, music and *joie de vivre*.

For the most part the city retains its neighborhoods' populations *toutes sortes de*. Such was ours where an ethnic mix included a preponderance of Frenchmen who left their elders' *quartier Francais* beginnings at the river. They came where the bayou once beckoned tribal Indians to hunt and fish in bountiful fields and waterways. Over two centuries later their offspring would run home breathessly with freshly unearthed arrow heads stashed in their overall pockets.

That generation was born in the Roaring 20s when energized "flappers" shimmied and shook to "Aint't We Got Fun?" We grew up in the Great Depression, whose name indicated it was a miserable time to live. We thought we were happy.

Though close to historic *faubourgs* St. John, Jackson and Pontchartrain our neighborhood had no name, as far as we knew. A speck on a map bordered by Bayou St. John, old

Orleans Canal and City Park, its curious topography has haphazarly intersecting "drives," "courts, "lanes" and "places" rather than streets. They are lined with shade trees and named for presidents Wilson, Harding, Roosevelt (Teddy), Taft, two obscure females Elaine and Olga, and such dewy-eyed addresses as Sherwood Forest, Bungalow and Flowerdale.

Life there was sustained by mom and pop corner grocery and meat market, drugstore (with a slot machine), two barber shops, a beanery and bakery, a couple of saloons and a snowball stand the proprietors of which, for the most part, resided on the premises. Also there were two schools, a church, motion picture theater, cemetery, orphanage, "filling station", amusement center with scenic railway, streetcar line and City Park all within walking distance from any house. The only out-of-step neighbor was a noisy can fabrication plant on the canal that operated on vampire schedule.

The rather new housing consisted mostly of Spanish bungalows, double cottages, stucco duplexes, "basement" styles and a couple of historic houses on the bayou. The dwellings are situated close to the sidewalks and behind small patches of grass. (Note: duplex elsewhere refers to a structure that contains two residences, but Orleanians say "duplex" to mean two dwelling units with one above the other. Two dwellings side by side that share a common wall is called a "double." No one knows why).

Neighborhood breadwinners included the ups, downs and in-betweens on the lifestyle scale - businessmen, mechanics, clerks, river pilots, lawyers, a baker, policemen, firemen, physicians, an undertaker, a cab company owner, a butcher, pharmacists, a dentist, an architect, salesmen, a theatrical impresario and one unrenowned motion picture actor, our next door neighbor.

Some neighborhood housewives played auction bridge-and attended oyster patty and lady finger luncheons regularly. They also cooked, mopped, sewed buttons on shirts, aired rugs, sorted socks, fed the pets, changed floor coverings and window curtains seasonally and administered smelly hot poultices to the chests of those with "congestion". A few were employed as nurses, secretaries or school teachers, and one, our neighbor, was a motion picture actress, who married silent film actor Conrad Nagel.

Morning Glory

There was a generous supply of front porches and small rear fenced yards that were decorated with clotheslines and Morning Glory vines. Popular pets were the German shepherd, English bull, collie and spitz, most of which died without ever visiting a vet. Richard had pet alligators. Alan had pet snakes. "Brother" had a room of floor-to-ceiling cages stocked with parrots and love birds. Nona Dee had a huge terrapin we could sit on. Garages were of sufficient size to age home brew in crocks next to the Essex, the family car. Roses, azaleas and Lady Slippers provided color. The can company's automations gave the neighborhood distinctive sounds. Roosters' crowing and hens' cackling could also be heard now and then.

Except for residents' cars there was little street traffic. What there was included the streetcar, mule-drawn vendors' wagons, the ice cream man's giant tricycle, and an occasional Toye Bros. Yellow cab for a feeble recluse who regularly visited her doctor.

The town had witnessed exciting central business area growth in the 20s, a kind of prosperity that wouldn't return for 30 years. Between those good times its inhabitants were content, friendly and of slow pace.

My recollections of life in the city then, and how its customs and traditions were practiced and revered, are cherished ones.

WHO WERE THOSE CREOLES? - FOR TRUE, *CHER*

Not very long ago passersby heard vestiges of Creole families speak melodious English with French phrases frequently tossed in. Prudent merchants hired bilingual clerks. The French connection is fundamental to New Orleans' being.

Nonc Alphonse or Tante Elodie might have been typical family members of a bygone clannish New Orleans society of whom the world knows little and understands less. Alphonse and Elodie never would have agreed that some definitions (even in dictionaries) accurately define Creoles in Nouvelle Orleans.

Early French families accepted one definition - theirs. Should the Creole himself know exactly what he is? *Me oui.* And that made it so.

Some historians and writers suggest that their colleagues treated facts loosely, and thereby contributed to confusion of the word's meaning in Louisiana. Recorded statements of Creoles (with a capital C) insist that a "Creole is a native Louisianian of French or Spanish ancestry, or both."

As late as 1886 Creole gentlemen attempted to identify themselves by organizing the Creole Association of Louisiana. They assembled - Theard, Romain, Layton, Sarrat, Lemarie', Laudumiey, Soniat, Claiborne, Villere, de Lassus, de Gruy and others - "to disseminate knowledge concerning their true origin and real character, and to promote the advancement of the Creole race in Louisiana."

When perusing faded records of Charles T. Soniat, the association's notary, New Orleans historian Henry Rightor wrote: "I found upon a yellowed paper ... the idea of Mr. Soniat and his friends as to the true meaning of the word Creole ... the Louisiana Creole is one who is a descendant of the original settlers in Louisiana under the French and Spanish governments, or, more generally, one born in

Louisiana of European parents, and whose mother tongue is French."

A 20th century Creole, the senior Joseph Roger Baudier, left us a treasure of family vignettes he wrote in the New Orleans archdiocesan newspaper until his death in 1933. They were assembled for posterity by Leonard V. Huber in "Creole Collage - reflections on the colorful customs of latter-day New Orleans Creoles."

Baudier's engrossing tales reflect the Creole's whimsical spirit, an endowment of manners and customs that set them apart from their contemporaries. Consider their *cafetiere,* drip coffee pot. Who but a faithful Orleanian would drip his coffee drop by drop, tediously with traditional care, never pouring it until the brew has been finalized? *Grandmere* did it that way, as did *des bisaieulas*, great grandparents.

Firmly entrenched in the city Creoles mingled little with others and seldom married an outsider. When they did marry early German or Irish settlers many immediately translated the names of their mates to French, or pronounced them to sound French. Some names were misspelled to make them appear as French. They clung tenaciously to their mother tongue and were distressed that when the Americans came their children were taught to speak English in schools.

Crillo Was First

Oddly, it was the Spanish, residing in their *Nueva Orleans*, who influenced the French Creole moniker. Before the word was used in *Nouvelle Orleans* the invading Spaniards called their children *crillo* (cree-yo) which meant "children born in the colony." So, the French became Creoles, their word for it.

At an early age I heard French, and English spoken with a lyrical accent. The progenitor of my mother's paternal family was Charles Barrois, who was a young man in the city when it was called *Nouvelle Orleans*. He died in New

7

Orleans in 1785.

When my mother, her sister, brother and cousins were children the Barrois (Bar-wah) family discouraged their offspring from speaking French. However, frequently adults drifted into the mother tongue at the dinner table, much to the chagrin of my English/Irish grandmother who spent many nodding hours at her in-laws' dining table sipping wine and listening to "French bibble-babble."

Because classmates called the children "Bow-wows" the family accepted the pronunciation "Barris". However, they insisted on proper spelling and objected to the inversion of "oi" to "io" as in Barrios. In recent years my grandmother called a department store to inform them that she refused to pay her bill until her account name was changed from Barrios to Barrois. "And stop calling me Mrs. Bar-ee-os," she added.

Hump In Rear

In my time the home of my grandfather's sister, Marie Barrois Boesch, was family headquarters. It was a large "camelback" house with a second level "hump" in its rear. Residing there also were her husband Herman, daughters Thelma and Ora, Thelma's husband Pat and their son Bill, and her two spinster sisters, Blanche Nan and Sug, whose given name was Dora. On two occasions I was invited into "the hump" by the "old maid" aunts who had candy or cookies waiting. Their private quarters above the treetops were bright with sunshine that spotlighted crocheted handicraft.

A popular gathering spot in the house was the large round dining table where simmering spicy dishes were served with piping hot French bread. There was plenty of red-stained rice lumpy with shrimp and ham in a colossal iron pot on the stove.

Clad in the largest apron in the world that hung loosely around her generous girth from neck to knee, Blanche Nan smiled proudly as she served us. "There's lots more, Cher."

It is possible today to be served jambalaya whose rice is wet and pasty. But not then. Blanche Nan's jambalaya emerged *chaque grain separe* - each rice grain separated. The adults had wine with dinner. At age seven I took mine with water, sugar and flaked ice.

We dined on Blanche Nan's spectacular file' gumbo or daube (strips of boiled beef with herbs and vegetables, sometimes jelled), veal *panee* (meat dipped in egg and dragged through bread crumbs before frying), stuffed crabs, crawfish bisque (with seasoned crawfish meat stuffed in the crustaceans' heads and scooped out with one's fingers), eggplant stuffed with shrimp or ham. Sometime there would be stuffed mirliton, or *grillades* (smothered veal round cut in squares that were inundated in a thick, dark gravy) and grits with *pain de mais*, plain corn bread.

Food preparation was a major happening in the Frenchman's home. Preparing the main meal began shortly after breakfast. It began with a *roux* - onion, bell pepper, celery chopped and browned in pasty butter and flour mix, sometimes with tomato, all stirred in a big iron skillet. Later, that was added to and cooked with string beans, limas or whatever.

Soup by Osmosis

Often there was soup made of something handy, perhaps several leftover greens and beef chunks. If a child didn't like soup a small bowl of it was placed in front of him, as though osmosis might get it into him.

Dining was never hurried. The family sat at the table relating tales, laughing and sipping wine for an hour or longer. When the table was cleared dessert was served along with hot coffee, always *au-lait* (with milk). Blanche Nan poured steaming black coffee from its agate drip pot into a large sauce pot, then poured in milk and slowly brought the mix to a boil. The aroma drifted through the house.

When family members were placed in their chalky white tombs they took their language with them, but not their recipes. Wise cooks know that the sassiest jambalaya has chaurice, a distinctive hot sausage.

My mother passed on Blanche Nan's traditional dishes to the next generation, and introduced my German meat-and-potatoes father to many tastes. Shortly after they were married he asked, "What's that?" pointing to *des artichauts*. He ate them *a la vinaigrette* for the remainder of his life.

The French cooks' popular ingredients were not available in Louisiana, so they improvised. Through the years such improvisations weren't all of French doing. Spaniards mixed in their favorite pungent additives. Africans introduced distinctive ways to cook. The Choctaws acquainted early settlers with herbs and spices. Caribbean islanders added their touches. The sum total of their doings resulted in the gastronomic splendor known as "Creole cuisine" that is still with us.

The French also gave us All Saints Day outings at the cemeteries, *la Fete des Rois* (Kings' Day parties), the Carnival, the *soiree, immortelles* (everlasting metal memorial wreaths placed on tombs), French bread, and such romantic names as Adrienne, Clarisse, Paulette, Cleophas and Augustin, and engaging nicknames such as Titine, P'tit Boy, Doudouce.

Creole's entertained family members and friends in their parlors where Papa might have played violin and Tante Adenise the piano for dancing. At these *soirees* guests sipped wine and anisette and selected from trays of home-made sweets - pralines, caramels, peppermint drops, sugar plums and Creole brioche.

When a guest in a Creole family's home one writer observed their "constant vivacity and joyousness of life. From morning to night there is never a moment that is not filled with some amusement or gaiety or lighthearted performance of the daily task."

'Making the Market'

The French Market was an important destination in the housewife's life. When not in her herb garden gathering spices or in her kitchen stuffing sausage mixture into animal membranes Madame and Teen, the family cook, were "making the market" at what they called *Halle de Boucheries* selecting plump live chickens or fresh shrimp. Her husband, uncles, father and brothers were in their offices puffing cigars and reading newspapers through pince-nez spectacles. Many were desk people in managerial or clerical jobs, and always immersed in paperwork.

In mid-1920s the old French Market appeared much as it had for many years. When a small boy I accompanied my parents there to buy fish and fowl that was slaughtered on the spot, and creole tomatoes and okra (home grown and with small c). Initially the site was an Indian trading post that was developed into a crude mart established by the Spanish in 1791 and substantially improved by the French. Through the years it's appearance and function changed some, and more recently it was recreated into what it is today. "Tch-tch," Blanche Nan would sigh.

Even in seedy days, after most Creoles had moved from "Frenchtown" to Faubourg Marigny Downtown or to Madame Livaudais' old subdivision Uptown, the old market was a fun place to visit. It seemed all the watermelons in the world were there, and crates of Louisiana's lollapaloosa strawberries were piled higher than a boy.

Customers walked along a broad center aisle between stalls that were packed with vegetables including the dreaded beet and odious mustard green, said to make a boy strong - after some resistance. River breezes swept through the market's broad openess between fat columns.

The fish market was in a separate, enclosed building. There my mother inspected scaly fish corpses with bulging eyes and fins stiff as keels that rested on beds of chopped ice. I pinched my nose as we walked over a tile floor on a boardwalk that protected our shoes from hose water, melting ice and fishy drippings.

Sometimes we'd buy a turtle for *soupe a la tortue* which I carried in a brown paper bag after slaughter, or shrimp wrapped in newspaper.

Miraculously the old French Market has survived sophisticated marketing and a hurried culture.

TOT DISCOVERS PARENTS ARE CARNIVAL CRAZIES

As a tot I suspected that my parents were Carnival Crazies, later I discovered that the condition is genetic, like bone structure and hair texture.

When I was an infant, the Carnival was celebrated much as it had been the previous century. There were formal balls beginning after Christmas and colorful street pageants before madness and masking on the last day, Mardi Gras.

My favorite recollection of Mardi Gras is at about age 6. I knew something was astir that morning because the sun was shining and my mother was still in bed with a wet towel on her head and a thermometer in her mouth. "It's down to

100," she moaned to my father.

I stood beside her bed in my costume complete with oversized hat that rested on stupendous ears, and a toy pistol strapped to my waist. I was Hoot Gibson, they told me. My mother applied her rouge to my cheeks ("You need some color") and burnt cork to my eyebrows while supporting herself on one elbow. "You'd better leave now, Daddy," she said to my father. She kissed me, and added, "Catch me something," sighed, and dropped upon her pillow.

Five private Carnival clubs paraded in the streets then. Their floats were constructed on flatbeds with iron wheels, and pulled by white-robed mules that had the day off from city garbage wagon detail. Each team was prodded by white-robed, hooded men. At the three night parades their ghostly attire protected them from sizzling oil that spun from twirling flambeaux carried by others also clad in hoods and capes. Among colorful traditions were these light bearers, prancing as their torches shot flashes of light on the gilded floats. Often the fiery streaks came perilously close to masked float riders when carriers stooped to scramble for coins tossed by onlookers. Children were repeatedly warned to keep their heads down. "Duck, Junior, here come the flambeaux."

'The Big 10'

We watched all Carnival parades in front of a Lee Circle building that offered comfort station privileges. Present was "the Big 10" - my parents, Harold and Mae, and their friends, nine other couples and 20 or so of their children. All bore given names popular at the turn of the century - Horace and Ethel (Cox) Brignac, Harry and Maude (Flott) Doize, Charles and Odile (Villarrubia) Evans, George and Nina (Nicaud) Hecker, Clarence and Germaine (Laudumiey) Holloway, Wallace and Nina (Harvey) Nicaud, James and Louise (Garic) Toca, Sidney and Gladys (Cox) Toca and Paul and Una (Garic) Welty. They were extended family. Some had been friends in grammar school or were team mates in sandlot ball leagues. Some were related or had married into the families of others. All resided in the old neighborhood "back of town."

Frequently we jigged in the cold waiting for a parade, or ran to shelter from drizzling rain. Suddenly, a siren shrieked!

14

The parade was coming! The parade was coming!

First came the horses with huge heads held high, their strutting hooves clapping cobblestones with great thuds. Their drool sometimes dripped into a kid's hair. Or something might have plopped on a kid's shoe.

Policemen straddled roaring motorcycles whose sounds drowned cheers of the crowd and brassy blasts of the marching bands.

Chili Drizzled

On Mardi Gras, Rex, King of Carnival, was resplendent sitting high above us on a golden throne and waving a jeweled scepter. The crowds pushed forward. Chili drizzled on satin costumes.

Masked riders on horseback wore velvet capes, leggings and leather boots, and waved ribboned riding crops. They were very traditional. When the floats passed my father hoisted me to his shoulder and yelled the names of masked riders. They'd lean over and hand him satin bags filled with beads from Czechoslovakia, small china dolls from China and kaleidoscopes and rubber daggers. I gobbled a doughnut so I could hold a satin bag.

"Throw me somethin' mistah," we screamed.

A time came when children no longer accompanied their parents to parades. Some neighborhood girls were presented at Carnival balls. They had been revamped, wearing white gowns with their shoulders exposed and gloves above their elbows. Young men squirmed in starched shirts and stifling collars to watch the young ladies being escorted around a ballroom floor under blinding lights. After the ball young ladies slumbered, young men changed to overalls and climbed wearily onto their bikes to deliver *The Times-Picayune*.

We grew up, but not Carnival. It remains wild, wacky, weird, wonderful and crowded. The horses drool, cycles roar and riders toss trinkets.

It Was My Turn

Years later I would be at Lee Circle with Happy and our children and my parents with their friends and their grandchildren. I yelled to men on the floats who leaned over to hand me beads from Czechoslovakia and china dolls from China. A tot was on my shoulder with a wet cookie oozing from his hands. His sisters were Dutch Girls ensconced atop a ladder.

There were 10 or more parading clubs then, and soon afterwards more than 20. Some paraded across the river, some across the lake, others on suburban highways. There is more royalty in the New Orleans Carnival in a single week than the sum total of all British royalty since Egbert, King of Wessex.

At some point docile mules were replaced by noisy tractors. Floats were neonized, electrified, mechanized and oversized. Some float riders have abandoned Carnival's mystery and masking tradition by exposing their faces. The Czechs must have stopped making beads because riders now toss "pearls" from Taiwan.

On Mardi Gras street maskers begin to appear along St. Charles Avenue as early as 4 a.m. to secure front row observation patches that quickly broaden into camps with alfresco nap and dine space for families and friends.

Before Rex appears, marching groups energize the waiting crowds with brassy horns and clashing symbols. Marching men with bottles raised to blood-flushed faces offer female onlookers paper flowers for kisses.

Revelers shuffle in lines, miles of them, most clad in outlandish garb. Many wear less than little, displaying themselves shamelessly for the attention of onlookers. Applause, whistles, hoots, howls, shrieks and cameras encourage the brazen exhibitionists. Musical sounds come from everywhere.

Canal Street swells with waves of people linked by tens of thousands of others Uptown on the avenue and Downtown in the old French Quarter. Rue Bourbon is a bubbling stew of pretense and reality, hardly distinguishable one from the other.

From the beginning fatigued crowds greeted the final parading monarch at dusk on Mardi Gras. Comus, the Mystick Krewe, introduced Carnival mystique to the streets with a dazzling tableau on floats. That was in 1857.

In 1991 the New Orleans City Council passed an ordinance that required private clubs to open their memberships to the public. Members of Comus and two other exclusive parading organizations, Momus and Proteous, were also members of private clubs. These three with historical Carnival ties, challenged the ordinance and won their case. Even so, they elected not to participate in Carnival's public merrymaking.

Thus was the city's link to the origin of Carnival's float tableaux severed as 135 years of public participation by Comus came to an abrupt and regrettable end.

With the public demise of Comus a bewildered public is never certain when the street party is supposed to end. There is no shimmering beauty in the dark, a final bit of pomp and pagentry, a fitting climax. By late evening frolickers are out in the streets hanging on but decelerated, hoarse, tired, tipsy, prone in public garden beds or snoozing standing up, as though searching for an end.

The next morning the town buzzes with traffic, slowed somewhat by a preposterous amount of trash, much of which has already been removed. Some motorists go directly to their offices for more coffee. Some go to churches to receive traditional Ash Wednesday smudges to remind them how foolishly they behaved the day before.

Priests smear crosses of ashes on their foreheads. They close their eyes. Their heads thump, abdomens churn, legs ache. They're so sorry. Mea culpa.

They remember until next year.

DECEASED ARE ALL AROUND US LIKE GOOD NEIGHBORS

Through the centuries New Orleans has been a place of enchanting customs. One more solemn than others introduced by Creoles is a public expression of reverence. On All Saints' Day Orleanians travel en masse to deliver floral tributes to deceased loved ones.

Among childhood memories none is more vivid than those that place me in a cemetery celebrating the holiday and holy day following Hallowe'en (Holy Eve).

Cemeteries are all around us, and walled, swept and landscaped as are properties of good neighbors. Such hallowed spaces are never referred to as graveyards. In New Orleans there are no graveyards of marble markers on grassy hills. There are no grassy hills.

Burials are a fascinating part of the town's history. The unrenowned of the initial inhabitants were buried near fortifications at city limits, and during fever epidemics many

corpses were tossed in the river. The renowned were buried in the church garden or beneath the cathedral's sanctuary floor. The colonists soon found underground burial unacceptable. Drenching rains and howling winds that swept the river into town literally upset the tranquil rest of loved ones. Walled cemeteries and above-ground tombs like those in Paris became a more appropriate final domicile.

Louis All Over

Many of the cemeteries are named for saints. The cathedral, a street, a fort that once protected city limits, an historic hotel and a total of three cemeteries (numbers 1,2 &3) were named for Saint Louis, New Orleans' patron. He was France's King Louis IX at age 11. Sovereign, warrior, saint he was declared "every inch a king," and canonized by the Church in 1297, 27 years after his death.

The more illustrious - in some cases notorious - the citizen the more magnificent his tomb, so that many tombs are outdoor art. The best European and local sculptors, sometimes architects, were commissioned to design then.

Less illustrious among the deceased were offered eternal rest in vaults fashioned into the cemeteries' brick walls. These are stacked one above the other full height of the wall, the top-of-a-ladder distance from the ground. These crypts are called "ovens" because they appear much like ovens into which bakers shoved their French bread loaves.

Hallowed Spots

These tombs and "ovens" are venerable spots. Even today you might see an elderly woman crossing herself with bowed head as she enters a cemetery, dutifully clutching floral bouquets wrapped in green tissue for Papa and Mama.

I recall seeing entire families out together in their Sunday best on All Saints Day. The men wore broad brim felt hats and black three piece suits with gold watch chains spanning their abdomens. All sported monogrammed belt buckles. The women wore their finest dresses and hats trimmed with feathers. The most recently widowed wore veils. Boys wore shirts with big collars, short woolen pants, high socks, and shoes that sparkled with waxy shines. Girls wore voluminous bow ribbons in their hair, dresses with broad sashes, and black patent leather shoes.

Outside the cemeteries the atmosphere was that of a carnival with hawkers offering candy, hot dogs, flowers and taffy. Always there was music, perhaps a clarinetist blowing soulful sounds or a drummer with an upturned hat on the *banquette.*

Year after year, from tyke to teen, I was dutifully present but uncertain why.

The time came when I understood that children before me became adults and took their children to the cemeteries as their parents had taken them. Only families in New Orleans did this. It was tradition - like the Carnival.

Before that awareness I ran between the freshly white-washed tombs, chasing small cousins or being chased by them. Our parents, their cousins and in-laws sat on iron benches, chattering in whispers at "the Planchard's place," my great grandmother's family tomb.

'No Damn Good'

The men often argued politics. "I tell you, Harold, the man is no damn good. He's not worth a red copper cent."

The women arranged and rearranged flowers. "Those were her favorites, pink roses. Oh, well, she is out of her misery. Ummmm-mmmph. Poor Cousin Tot."

As my father dusted my clothing free of smudges of fresh whitewash on the tombs, I peered at their walls trying to imagine what the interior was like. Could Tot hear them?

Children sat on the tomb steps licking candied apples on sticks and staring at the inscriptions on the marble tablet. All of those people, all of those names, all great great grandparents, great great aunts and uncles. All so quiet.

When the apples were gone we sometimes had pralines. From our hands we slurped water that was drawn from a faucet on a pipe that popped up from the ground. Visitors filled flower vases there.

Before leaving, young and old knelt on the tomb's granite steps or on the brick path, bowed their heads and whispered rapid prayer. When we stood, women hugged and kissed all of the children and each other.

Like Tante Ema

A final comment might have been, "Look, how big he's getting." Or, "Oh, Inez, she has hair just like Tante Ema." For years I thought they spoke of "Tony Mah." I wondered who he was.

Outside the cemetery pilgrims shuffled on crowded *banquettes*, some going in, some coming out through big iron gates beneath an arch that spelled out in iron the cemetery name.

I observe the tradition of All Saints' Day, but no longer visit three cemeteries. Now I visit just one, sometimes two. And alone.

I don't eat candied apple-on-a-stick. There are no children running between the tombs, no men talking politics, no powder-scented ladies to be hugged by. I read the tombs' inscriptions. My eyes glisten and burn.

EVERYBODY IS SOMEPLACE, BUT WHERE?

New Orleanians are probably the only people in the country - maybe the world - who are not certain exactly where they are in conventional terms.

They do not locate position or express direction in regular geographical jargon. When moving about in the city their orientation is not based on where the sun rises or sets. Their directional language is unique. And for the visitor, mystifying.

Like their mannerisms, orientation and direction took hold of the populace long ago. And without explanation.

The people in New Orleans travel lakeward, riverward, Uptown and Downtown. The reason is because that's the way it is. That's the way it has always been, way back when directional labels included "swamp side" and "woods side." Early French residents described their general location as being bounded "on the east by The Floridas, on the South by the Gulf of Mexico, and on the north and west by the unknown lands."

However strange to others the natives' directional system makes perfect sense to them. Here is the system: Canal Street is the original dividing line between the old town and the new American side of town. What is on the older side of this neutral territory (the French Quarter) is called Downtown. The portion of town on the opposite side of the free space is called Uptown.

River & Lake

Also, Canal Street extends from the Mississippi River to Lake Pontchartrain, the river is its lower extremity, and the lake its upper. The street's two terminal points - river and lake - provide the names of the remaining two directions. Orleanians use Uptown, Downtown, river and lake rather than the common north, south, east and west as geographic locations. However, the Orleanians' directional terms are not synonyms for customary geographic language. They are substitutes. Attempting to match them is useless.

Much of the city is enveloped in the convoluted river's bend and street patterns follow the river's contours so that north, south, east and west can change depending upon where one is in relation to the river.

Some street labels create paradoxical situations such as the relationship between two major thoroughfares Claiborne and Carrollton. Consider that Canal Street's intersecting streets are labeled South So-and-So on its Uptown side and North So-and-So on its Downtown side. One of these is Claiborne Avenue, named South Claiborne on its Uptown side, North Claiborne on its Downtown side. Another is South Carrollton Avenue and North Carrollton. A disturbing thing happens to South Carrollton on its way to the river. At a point Uptown South Carrollton Avenue crosses South Claiborne Avenue. It doesn't matter that it can't, it does.

Local Mumpsimus

Maybe street signs in New Orleans are not always trustworthy. No one is certain. Through the years the city's streets department has painted and repainted miles of signs for a street named for U.S. President Millard Fillmore. The municipal spelling is "Filmore" with one L. The Post Office, newspapers, the telephone company and even the people who live on Fillmore accept Filmore as proper. It has become a local mumpsimus.

In my youth an Uptown kid leaving home for Canal Street by streetcar knew he was "traveling Downtown" and the Downtown kid riding to Canal street knew he was "traveling Uptown." The business section was called Downtown by Uptowners and Uptown by Downtowners.

For many generations a kid standing on Canal Street with

his back to the river could travel in three directions - Uptown, lake, and Downtown. But not riverward. There was no bridge in the area then.

Shunned Ferry

There was a ferry at Canal Street but an East Bank kid wouldn't have considered taking the ferry to the West Bank. At least not until he was an adult and married to a West Bank girl. Then he would have Thanksgiving dinner at his in-laws house on the West Bank and attend their funerals there. Only on such occasions would he have taken the ferry to the West Bank.

A kid on the West Bank, on the other hand, often came over on the ferry to the East Bank where the big high schools, big parks, big banks, big hotels, big hospitals, big department stores and palatial movie houses were.

That's all changed now, east bankers travel to the West Bank regularly by way of the Crescent City Connection, a name for the bridge submitted by a schoolgirl. They visit Grannypoo in the nursing home or pick up hot sausage on sale at a supermarket.

It's interesting to note that when a kid stands at the "foot" or "head" of Canal street (natives use both terms) at the river he is looking across the river somewhat easterly at the West Bank. But if the kid rides a paddlewheeler upriver to a point near the U.S. Trade Zone wharves and looks across the river he is looking directly south, though at the same West Bank.

When the boat travels farther upriver beyond Audubon Park at a point near South Carrollton Avenue if the kid looks at the West Bank he is facing due west.

What makes things seem different than they are is the river showing off it's "beautiful crescent," the one that had Bienville in such a tizzy.

The truth is that until the federal interstate system was built Orleanians never heard words like east and south.

Possibly New Orleans was the last city in the country to have its share of interstate completed. Though no one ever admitted it, I suspect that sign painters fell victim to relentless migraines when attempting to figure out directional labels, hence the delay in construction. Then came a Texas investor who named the huge swampy property he bought New Orleans East. No matter what the signs read we all know it's Downtown.

Note to visitors: If a native recommends a seafood restaurant at the city's West End, there is no need to cross the bridge to the West Bank. West End is on the East Bank. You don't have to know why.

It's best not to get lost in New Orleans. For that very reason many older natives who reside on the East Bank seldom, if ever, venture to the West Bank by way of the grand "new" bridge. They protest that Grannypoo should have stayed where she was.

One senior couple we'll call A.J. and Joyce, native east bankers, claim never to have crossed over the "new" bridge. Their reason: "We tried once but couldn't find the up ramp from where we were. No. Neither of us has ever been on the West Bank. Not in our lives. Never."

Orleanians are steadfastly provincial.

WUTCHAMACALLIT - ORLEENZE, AWLINZ

New Orleanians are likely to be the only people in the world who hear multiple pronunciations of their city's name. When the city was no longer called Nouvelle-Orleans the pronunciation of its American name got caught up in a pro-fusion of dialects. Natives in each section of town and out-of-towners had their personal way of pronouncing it without the slightest care that their version was unlike others.

Through the years I've changed the way I pronounce the name of my city three times. One might wonder about such indecision, but the native doesn't. The native ignores it.

Say aloud the names of the following cities: PENSACOLA, MEMPHIS, NATCHEZ, ST. PAUL, NEW ORLEANS.

No doubt you pronounced the first four correctly. But are you certain about the fifth? You should be because however you said it is acceptable, though not necessarily popular.

Here are various ways to pronounce New Orleans:

NEW ORL-YUNZ. This is not the most common way but is popular among some natives and literati. As fifth graders in Our Lady of the Holy Rosary School's musical extrava-ganza we were taught a song that went, "New Orl-yunz, New Orl-yunz you're such a grand old town, I'll tell the world around ..." That's when I first heard that pronuncia-tion.

NEW OR-LEE-ENZ. This three syllable treatment has long been around and grows in popularity. You hear it at the New Or-lee-enz Country Club. (Some say New Orl-yunz Country Club). You might hear a university professor say New Or-lee-enz during a TV interview. Usually, he's not a native. Recent mayors said New Or-lee-enz.

NEW OR-LINZ. This one is widely used and has been passed down for generations in many families. It is not con-fined to use in one section of town. Chances are you will hear TV reporters and anchor people saying New Or-linz.

But after they are here for a while you may hear them pronouncing it another way. One is free to choose.

NOO AW-LINZ. A sound variation of the above this is used by natives who do not mention Rs in their speech. They will say "faw" as in "How faw is it?" and "caw" as in "Can you pick me up in ya caw by my mama's house on Sad-dy evenin' at arown two?" And there's a clue. People who say Noo Aw-linz do not usually recognize afternoons. "Mawnins" end at noon and "eve-nins" begin sometime after lunch and last until dark which is called "nighttime."

NEW OR-LEENZ. This pronunciation absolutely is never used by natives or long-time residents. Until more recently it was strictly Yankee or foreign talk and at one time almost always was heard in motion pictures. On the Johnny Carson show several years ago this pronunciation was dropped worldwide almost overnight. When celebrated New Orleans musicians appeared on Carson's show, and were asked, "How do you say New Or-leenz?" The response was, "Noo Aw-linz." Since then movie characters, U.S. presidents and foreign dignitaries say "Noo Aw-linz."

N'AWLINS. Rather recent and seldom heard is this style promoted by local media people. You may go through life without ever hearing it but you'll see it in print, especially in headlines where space is restricted.

OR-LAY-AWN. Natives say this only when referring to the Orleans Club, and is the French pronunciation. Only a visitor would call it the Or-leenz Club.

Note: The native does say Or-leenz when referring to Or-leenz Parish, Or-leenz Levee Board or Or-leenz Street. If the Orleans Levee Board ever made the national news Dan Rather would likely refer to it as the Or-linz Levee Board.

VOODOO, GRIS-GRIS, CHARMS, BLACK MAGIC & OTHER NONSENSE

Nobody kept records so it's anybody's guess when voodooism came to New Orleans.

The art of hexing likely was introduced when practitioners came here from the French possessions of Santo Domingo and Martinique. The Caribbean was a voodoo hatchery, and some savvy blacks there excelled in the practice.

By the time Spain governed *Nueva Orleans* voodoo was widely practiced by "queens" and "doctors" who pursued their art seriously. Essentially theirs was a harmless superstition but the Creoles felt intimidated by it. They didn't really, truly believe in it, but ...

Spooky Beliefs

It became such a social to-do that by 1782 Spanish Governor Bernardo de Galvez ordered a halt in importation of blacks from the islands. Life in *Nueva Orleans* was unsafe because of their spooky beliefs, he declared.

Within a few years after the sale of the territory Americans lifted the restriction. Voodooism swept through the city and surrounding areas.

Superstitions are deeply rooted. Even today the most stable host would request that you remove your hat from a bed, and his sophisticated

wife might steer you in the proper direction if you attempt to leave by a door other than the one through which you entered. And please, do not open an umbrella indoors. Why? It's all bad luck.

Our neighborhood was populated with bits of French, German, Irish, Italian, Spanish cultures and one Greek family. Folklore was as plentiful as poisonous mushrooms after a rain. After learning to walk and speak we learned never to rock an unoccupied rocker with hand or foot. To this day I am not sure what happens when a person rocks an unoccupied rocker with his foot or hand. I never do that.

'Roomatizz' Cure

Particularly in the "country" people often treated their own malfunctions magically. They rubbed raw potatoes and lotions made of rattlesnake oil on their aches. "Roomatizz" pain disappeared promptly when cut up potatoes tied in a cloth were applied to the painful area. A rub with a brass ring cured infection.

My father, after all else failed, rubbed my confounded styes with his gold wedding band. He surmised that if brass could do it gold certainly could. The discomfort would increase.

Tea made from roots of anything could sweat the fever from almost anybody. Even red pepper was a tea base. When teething made a baby cranky dried swamp lilies were bagged and tied around its neck. Sometimes red flannel bags with God-only-knows-what in them (some suspected animal bones) were draped over a bawling infant's neck. That was enough to frighten an infant and his parents into silence.

There were varied ways to administer voodoo. You could hire a "doctor" to put a curse on someone. The victim's name was written three times on paper upon which a black candle was burned. That would do it. An order for sudden death required a photograph of the target.

The Gris-Gris

My grandmother told me that when she was pregnant, a woman who had been my grandfather's "intended" paid "some crazy woman to put a gris-gris on me." One day my grandmother found a small bag hanging on the alley gate. "It was one of those foolish gris-gris things with my name written on a folded note with dried leaves and flower petals and a tiny baby doll in it - like you'd find in a king cake. And rancid lard."

"What did you do, Mumzie?"

"I showed it to your grandfather and told him that the woman was unstable and meant to harm our baby. I reported her to the priest and asked him to pray for us."

"And what happened?" I asked.

"Seven months later, right on schedule, I had your Nana."

"So what does that prove?"

"That proves the power of prayer," she snapped.

Charms were multitudinous. Mademoiselles slept with a strand of a young man's hair in a handkerchief under their pillows to turn friendships into romances. They also slept with their beaux pictures under their pillows and stashed thimbles wrapped in silk in their pockets, all with a fervent hope that they would soon be married. For speedier results they carried a picture of St. Joseph in their purses. Such devotion assured marriage within six months.

If a pesky salesman came to the door with his foot inside the shutters salt was tossed on him. He never returned.

The dog's howling kept you awake? You simply smeared some of your own sweat in your hand and rubbed it on the animal's nostrils. There was always the risk the dog would find a new master.

To cast spells practitioners stored shells, lizards, dried weeds, oils, hoot owl heads, pebbles and images in small bags.

One cult leader succeeded another. The beloved Sante Dede was followed by the most famous of New Orleans voodoo queens, the Big Bugaboo of Mumbo Jumbo, Marie Laveau. Her tomb in St. Louis Cemetery No. 1 is a popular tourist attraction. A free mulatto native of New Orleans, Laveau lived with a man (some say her husband) whose name is inscribed on her tomb.

In the twilight of her life her flock asked that she step down from voodoo royalty. After a new queen replaced her she attended daily Mass at St. Louis Cathedral looking penitential and kneeling for long periods. Until weary with age she mixed traditional prayer with her magic.

In 1875, when she no longer appeared in public, writer George W. Cable persuaded her to be interviewed. He wrote: "I once saw her in extreme old age .... when she lived in a small adobe cabin but a step or two from Congo Square ... quaking with feebleness in an ill-looking old rocking chair, her body bowed, and her wild, gray witch's tresses hanging about her shriveled yellow neck. They said she was one hundred years old." She died a short time later.

Her magic was nothing like ours 55 years later. As small boys, we stood in a friend's basement when pouring rain robbed us of play time. We performed an authentic old New Orleans "rain stopper" trick. With our arms protruding out the door into the rain we placed two crossed matches on the walk and poured salt over them. When the salt disappeared the rain would stop. More often than not it worked. We were amazed at our power.

For a Nosebleed

Edma Pierce Nothacker remembers remedies handed down through generations in her French family. "To stop a nosebleed you hung a string with a key tied to it around your neck. I remember the frustration of trying to hold an ice bag on my nose with that danged key hanging there while I sopped up the blood with a towel."

What happened? "It just continued bleeding."

Edma's mother, Aimee Pitre Pierce, learned many remedies in rural Lafourche Parish. She claimed not to be superstitious, but was uncomfortable about certain omens like an owl hooting in the day. *"Le hibou* - the owl - hooting in daylight meant that a member of the family would die."

The tale spread about a family who heard an owl hooting in the daylight. An elderly man in the family got out his shotgun and shouted, 'Gonna shoot me a owl there, yes, kill him off, yes, before somebody in family he die.' BANG! The owl fell out of the tree. The old man dropped dead.

Edma's armoire superstition: Flip a pancake atop the armoire and leave it there for good luck. Cajuns performed this ritual on *"fete de Dieu"* - God's Day- the feast of Christ the King. There was a chance you'd also see a creature with big red eyes, pointed nose, long tail and hair all over it. To save oneself from the thing a person simply tossed a frog at it. Frogs are plentiful in Louisiana bayou country.

French Quarter shops today sell voodoo potions and grisgris charms. You may find the proprietor done up in voodoo de rigueur to impress the shopper. It's a good idea to buy a little trinket.

'AH GOT FA-RESH MUSTIT GA-REENS, LAY-DEEEEE'

The street vendors' sing-song summons could be heard a block away as they made their way through our neighborhood and into others until their wagons were empty.

Much of street traffic in New Orleans' in the early 30s was the truck farmers' mule-drawn wagons from which they sold their produce. The "vegetable man" might have been a sturdy youth with muscled arms or a bent, frail man with gnarled hands and liver spots. He sat on a wooden plank covered with a worn blanket, and his head rose above the mule's rump, offering an unobstructed view of housewives waiting on the sidewalk.

Behind him, under a canvas canopy, were baskets filled with whatever his garden offered that morning. We called him "the vegetable man" as though that were his given name, but his load frequently included fruits and berries. He featured them in his melodious call. "Ah got berrrrries, laaadeee, fa-resh blackberrrrry, ripe and strawbaaaaary laadeeee and jooocy aw-range so sweet right offen the tree, laaadeeee."

Water for Dolly

When the mule turned her head and looked forlornly with big brown eyes from under a floppy straw hat at her master, he'd carry a pan of water to the animal and wipe her brow with a wet rag.

A kid could pet the old mule, whose name was Dolly, and offer it fresh-plucked grass, as his mother scanned the wagon's load. She bartered for the lowly string bean. "Ummm. How much are your snap beans?"

"Dime a pound. Nice too, lady."

"They look old."

"They owniest 'bout tree, or fo' ow-waz ole, ma'am."

"I'll take two pounds. And a nice bunch of turnips. No,

34

not that one, that one."

The mule moved on - clippety-clop, clippety-clop. The big pan scale swung on its chain as the wagon lumbered along.

On summer afternoons "the watermelon man" came with "sa-weeeet, jooo-cyy, watamel-unz - raaad and so sweeet."

He was followed by "the snowball man." In the center of

his wagon was a chunk of ice as big as an iceberg. It was covered with canvas upon which rested his ice scraper. Syrups in large squirt bottles rattled in their racks when the wagon moved. There were so many flavors - 5 in all - a kid could hardly decide which to take.

Freezing Nose

"The snowball man" created coolers right before our eyes, scraping the ice and packing it into glasses we brought from home. A kid's teeth froze from the snowy treat, and sometimes his nose.

Often a boy accompanied "the snowball man." He sat on the wagon seat holding the mule's bridle reins, and slurping a snowball. "He's just advertisement," mothers told us.

What a lucky kid riding in a wagon eating snowballs. He could have all the flavors without spending three coppers. Being an advertisement was unbridled fun.

On Fridays "the fish man" came. He sold speckled trout, shrimp and sometimes crabs. On Fridays, as surely as the sun and moon appeared, New Orleans families had seafood gumbo and fried fish, or shrimp-stuffed eggplant for dinner. But never catfish. City folk considered catfish "dirty." This baffled me because Mumzie ate catfish. "As sweet as candy," she told me when I refused to eat it.

If your mama missed "the fish man" the family had vegetable soup, tuna salad in a tomato and cucumber with vinaigrette dressing for dinner.

'Chim-il-ly Sweep'

Singing vendors were all over town but specialists such as the "chimney sweepers" traveled where they were most needed - in the Quarter, and in old Downtown and Uptown neighborhoods.

These men, who traveled in pairs, wore tuxedo attire of a sort and stove-pipe hats over woolly caps. They carried rope and course straw that was bound to poles that were used to free the stacks of soot and nests. They walked on the *banquettes* singing, "Chim-il-ly sweep, chim-il-ly sweep."

In the days of fireplace heat, wood stove cooking and boiling the family wash over a grate, the "kindling man" was a popular street vendor. He called, "Ah got woods and kindlin'. Git all yah woods, heah."

There were knife sharpeners, umbrella repairmen, "clothes pole men," homemade candle vendors and "mops and brooms men." The latter carried their wares in back-packs held steady by straps around their heads. "Gotcha brum heah, ma'am. Gotcha brum and ya mop."

"The ice cream man" arrived in our neighborhood precisely at 3:15, just as we arrived home from school. He pedaled a tricycle outfitted with an insulated chest in which he kept small cups of ice cream, Popsicles and fudgesicles. We plunged our heads into the foggy coldness that rose from the chest when he popped it open. In a special bag tied to his waist he kept some seedy merchandise - tiny books featuring newspaper comic strip characters carrying on as they never did in the "Sunday funnies." Pornography was secretive in those days.

The *cala* vendors were only in the French Quarter. Black women attired in aprons and tignons sold Creole rice cakes from baskets on their arms. Also on Quarter *banquettes* were praline vendors dressed in "mammy" gingham who softly greeted passersby. *"Belles pralines, monsieur."*

The colorful street vendors vanished after World War 11. Suburbs and supermarkets were in.

WHEN NEIGHBORS VISITED ON THE STOOPS

In old New Orleans neighborhoods there are rows of small cottages called "shotguns". These Victorian dwellings that were popular near the turn of the last century because of their frugality, are being restored near the turn of another because of their charm.

They got their name because of their appearance.

Chances are that if a shotgun were fired through the front door its bullet would exit at the rear door without striking a wall. The four or five rooms follow one behind the other from *banquette* to backyard. A tiny bathroom off one side of a short hall offers the only private area in the plan.

Except for their exposures each side of the double dwelling is exactly the same, and share a common wall down its center. For the investor the design offered double for his money on a small lot when development space was scarce.

Smack on the *banquette* is the entry - two or three wooden treads flanked by a pair of boxed seats on each side leading to the door. Here families sat comfortably to "catch a breath of air" in summertime.

The front door often is accompanied by tall cypress shutters that offer privacy and air circulation through open front and back doors.

Under the Bed

The front room was a Victorian parlor with fireplace and separated from the second room by heavy double wooden sliding doors. The second room was intended to be part of a double parlor, and was also equipped with mantel, grate and colorful tiles on the hearth. As a family expanded the second room became Mama's and Papa's room. It was furnished with Victorian pieces highlighted by billowy mosquito netting that cascaded from the tester. There was a marble wash stand with china bowl and pitcher, a marble top dresser, mirrored armoire and rocking chair. Hidden under the bed was a porcelain hand painted chamber pot, a leftover from outhouse days but still convenient on chilly nights.

Next was a short hall and bath, an elaborate addition that replaced the backyard privy. Another bedroom also with fireplace was followed by the kitchen with wood-burning stove and built-in safe. A small room at the rear probably was heated by a kerosene heater. The rear yard was fenced and offered space for a mirliton vine, rosebushes, clotheslines and a dog. Or perhaps a goat that was a popular pet for boys who hitched homemade wagons to the animals. Also in the yard was a shed for wood storage, and grate and tub for boiling clothes.

Windows were hung with cypress "blinds" offering privacy from the neighbors whose windows and "blinds" were a narrow alley away. A high horizontal board fence kept all but extremely tall neighbors from view.

The facade boasted decorative dentals, spools and curlicues. In many instances only the fronts of the cottages were painted since sides and rear were hardly visible from the street. Both occupants shared two or three stocky chimneys along the roof ridge.

The Gate Bell

The wooden alley gates were equipped with porcelain knobs and pull chain bells. These were sounded by the "coal man," "kindling and wood man" and "ice man" who made deliveries through the alleys.

In winter months life in the little cottages must have been rather dreary, but in springtime and summer the houses offered a station for full family social calendar, night and day.

Family and friends gathered at the stoop that was never painted, but swept daily and scrubbed to a shine on Saturdays to assure splinter-free comfort. The family assembled after their bath, change of clothes and dinner to enjoy "the cool of the evening."

Cleaning the stoop on Saturday mornings was as faithfully practiced as scrubbing clothes and cooking red beans on Mondays and attending church on Sundays.

From the shed women came through the alley gates with metal pails of steaming hot water. They plunged large stiff-bristled brushes into the buckets, rubbed them with a bar of Octagon soap and scrubbed the steps in circular fashion, the same spot over and over until they were sheen clean. Buckets of cool rinse water washed away suds.

The foamy water streamed across the *banquettes* and into the cobbled street. Entire blocks were flooded with frothy bubbles, some airborne. In the French Quarter the bubbles burst on passing streetcars.

Dozens of women did their chores simultaneously on Saturdays. All wore large aprons and knotted scarfs on their heads as they scrubbed, then swept wet *banquettes* that glistened in the sunshine. "Be-AT-tris, bring that there brush. You missed this heah part."

This went on in all of the old neighborhoods, wherever there were shotgun cottages with stoops - in Marigny, Treme, Irish Channel, Uptown, Downtown and Algiers.

After dinner, in early evening, as others sat on swings and rockers on galleries and porches, shotgun dwellers sat on their stoops.

A family might consist of Papa, Mama, Billy Boy and Della, and Uncle Charlie and Aunt Pansy who might have lived around the corner. Mr. Edgar and Miss Pauline came from four houses down. Miss Pauline's mother, Old Lady Gavasse, might not be coming. Her feet were "all swolled up" again.

The children played "May I?" or "Fate" (New Orleans hide and seek). The women were served lemonade. The children were treated to snowballs from "Mr. Justin's place" around the corner. The men drank draft beer.

Fill the Pitcher

There were saloons within walking distance of all houses in any neighborhood. The Papa sent the most trustworthy eldest boy to Mister Justin's to "fill-a pitcha." The boy took along an aluminum pitcher to carry back cold sudsy beer to

41

the Papa who poured it into glasses for the men present and a tankard for himself. In a short time the boy was back at the saloon for a refill.

At some point Miss Pauline might have gone into the parlor to play the piano without ever being asked. She would play without sheet music, and with all fingers.

The evening ended when the Mama stood, fluttered her cardboard fan from the funeral home furiously for a last gasp of outdoors, and exclaimed, "Ah'm tired." She awakened the Papa by tapping her fan on his head. "Della, lock the blinds," she would command as she swept through the parlor and into her boudoir, the first one with the towering tester bed and prie-dieu.

The last sound of the evening was the Mama's call to the household: "I hope everybody said their prayers ... kneeling."

The Papa's croaking snores lulled all to sleep.

In the darkness eerie shapes of light shimmied on the walls and ceiling in the Mama's bedroom. The ghostly apparition was sparked by a flickering vigil light before the image of St. Michael on the mantel. St. Michael, the Mama told her family, kept them safe.

Residents in the cottages were of a special New Orleans caste - God-fearing, proud, industrious, independent, reliable and fully absorbed in family.

ROARING STREETCAR INTRODUCED YOUNGSTERS TO THEIR CITY

There was a time in New Orleans when streetcars offered not only economical transit but adventure for a kid with seven cents. It was a tingling thrill to be master of his fate, off to the dentist, alone, and riding the streetcar up front with the motorman.

The two men operating the trolley were dressed as twins in matching blue serge uniforms. They wore imposing caps with ventilated crowns and brass badges above patent leather visors. Heavy white gloves, black shoes and white socks completed the ensemble. Both frequently peeked at their vest pocket watches. Trolley commanders always had the exact time.

The conductor let passengers in on the rear platform, clicked out change from a coin bank strapped to his waist, yanked a meter cord to register fares and rang a bell to sound the all clear.

Up front was the trolley's hero, the motorman. His skills with handles and pedals were a marvel to watch. He steered the trolley with a handle, stopped it with a handle and manipulated the door with a handle.

A young passenger resting his arms on the sill of the big open window next to the motorman felt the wind sting his face and whip his hair. A big-eared kid felt as though he were sailing.

Knotted Fare

My mother tied carfare, two pennies and a nickel in one end of my handkerchief. Boys always carried handkerchiefs. "Now don't untie it until you're ready to board the streetcar to come home, you hear?"

She handed me two more pennies and a nickel for immediate fare, and an additional quarter and a few nickels for a soda on Canal Street and a Milky Way at the palatial Loew's State.

Soon my friends and I were aboard the "City Park" car on the platform with the motorman. The car chugged at first, its trolley making popping sounds - carrrrracck - and then it rushed away, faster, rocking on its tracks tilting from side to side like a big buggy.

We swayed from side to side with the motorman who stomped the floor pedal to sound a bell. Clang! Clang! Clang! Watch out, everybody. You on the bike, you with the puppy in the street watch out. The streetcar is coming. Run dog, run. We crossed the old bridge across the bayou and roared into neighboring territory of long rows of small houses.

Then we made a thrilling turn into palm-studded Ursulines Avenue that was carpeted with bright green grass. Shrubs behind iron picket fences circled stately houses with broad verandas, half hidden by big green canvas awnings. Soon we turned into narrow streets without trees or a single blade of grass. House closely followed house, nearly wall-to-wall and sometimes sharing a wall. Now and then a narrow alley separated them.

Wash Hung Out

I remember that in the early 30s dwellers in a fading French Quarter hung out their wash on balconies for all to see and aired tattered bedding over balcony rails. Housewives gathered their hair in pins atop their heads, and propped infant children on their hips as they gossiped on the *banquettes*. Sometimes they yelled out in a foreign tongue to another child. Dusty white dogs sniffed at street vendors' shoes.

Gutters were full with idle water. House paint was flaked. Barefooted men in undershirts sat on stoops playing cards. They worked nights at laborious tasks.

I can recall that my fanny ached from rocking on the hard

wooden seats as the streetcar sped through a long narrow street, seldom picking up a passenger, never letting one off. It turned sharply passing within inches of a saloon's broad tin canopy that extended from the building's facade to the edge of the *banquette*. Would the streetcar ever smack into one of its slender poles? Never. At Canal Street we jumped from steps that unfolded when the door flaps opened, and were off and running to the K&B soda fountain. Behind the long marble counter three women with tiny caps atop lofty coiffures made chicken salad sandwiches, poured coffee and scooped ice cream. We spun on swivel stools until one of them asked what we wanted.

Sucked Straws

Chocolate sodas were special, the best, the sign said. We sucked on long straws until the glasses were dry, until they no longer made a sound. It was swell. Outside we hurried past the big stores through crowds of people walking in all directions, coming and going in and out of glass doors. The men wore suits and hats, and the ladies wore dresses, silk stockings, high heeled shoes, hats and gloves.

At the far end of Canal Street we crossed to the Loew's State, about as close to magnificence an ordinary kid could get in New Orleans. A banner hung across its marquee: "It's Cool Inside." The coolness was a new summertime miracle that appeared only in the Loew's State, Saenger and Orpheum theaters and a few big Canal street stores. It felt as though we were packed in ice with fans blowing on us. It was swell.

For 25 cents we saw Andy Hardy and his girlfriend, Polly Benedict, and a Laurel & Hardy short subject, a cartoon, the news, the coming attractions and an educational "travel" film about some strange place at the end of the world.

When the educational film came on we went to visit "the candy lady" in the lobby. She had Hershey bars and licorice.

We sipped ice cold water from the grand fountain, then walked down the broad curving staircase. Velvety golden fabric-covered walls shimmered in the light of a massive chandelier that hung high overhead. We caught glimpses of ourselves in huge mirrors that hung on the wall alongside blownup photos of Jean Harlow, Johnny Weismuller and Wallace Beery. It was swell.

Back in our loge seats we munched candy while having a second helping of Laurel & Hardy comedy.

Ahead was the fun streetcar ride home. The streetcar displayed large warning signs over the front and rear platforms: "Do Not Spit Upon the Floor Under Penalty of the Law." I never witnessed such a social gaffe. Dozens of ads for popular products were framed above the windows for the trolley's full length. I knew by heart messages from Old Gold cigarettes and Juicy Fruit gum. The whole town knew that nine out of 10 screen stars used Lux.

'Beauty Seats'

Those who sat in regular seats swayed from side to side as the car raced along its tracks. At the front and rear were horizontal bench seats where passengers sat shoulder-to-shoulder with their backs against the windows. They swayed back and forth instead of from side to side. They were as though on exhibition in "beauty seats."

"Beauty seat" passengers often bumped knees with and were slammed in the faces by packages of standing passengers who held onto porcelain handgrips that hung from an overhead rod. Only men stood holding the grips. All "ladies" sat. Men rose to give them their seats. It was a courtesy, not a law like the one prohibiting spit on the floor.

There were times when I traveled on the streetcar alone into other neighborhoods to visit my grandmother on Esplanade or cousins Uptown. During such trips I saw bits of the city's past that appeared to be new.

There were grand oaks along historic Esplanade where houses were large but close, and where families resided for generations. People sat out on galleries above the treetops, rocking. Windows were tall and narrow, and always open with gauzy curtains blowing out over the gray planks of the galleries. Banana trees, elephant ears and crepe myrtles thrived along the edges of clam shell driveways.

When traveling to Uptown a Downtown kid got a transfer, a slip of blue paper with holes punched in it and tiny print nobody ever read. You knew you were a seasoned traveler when you used a transfer and changed trolleys. Approaching Uptown from Canal a boy was treated to the "business district."

Clickety-clak. Clickety-clak. The streetcar passed skyscrapers, one with 19 floors, tallest in town. On route were handsome buildings such as the St. Charles Hotel. At Lee Circle a bronze likeness of a Confederate general atop a fluted shaft rose from a circular hill. Nearby was a lofty columned structure set high above a double set of marble steps on terraced ground. At this main public library (since demolished to make room for progress) the street became an avenue, broader, greener and shady from trees whose moldy branches made a canopy over the street.

Occasionally, when the trolley car passed close to huge azalea and camellia bushes I'd stretch out an arm to snatch a blossom, as did others.

Impressive Homes

Set back far from shaded sidewalks on manicured lawns were many of the city's most impressive houses, mansions built by prominent citizens such as Samuel Gilmore, Lawrence Fabacher, Charles Allgeyer, Isidore Newman, A.B. Wheeler, Henry Dart, M.L. Whitney, Robert Moore and others.

Along the way were rows of formal hedges, tall iron picket fences, arbors and fountains, broad porte cocheres guarded by stone lions, marble steps, verandas whose rockers were outfitted with starched white coverlets, railed widows' walks, turrets, garrets, dormers, great chimneys, balconies and magnificent doors that giants could fit through.

Except for a gardener or uniformed chauffeur there was never a person around. No one was ever seen rocking on the grand porches, or coming and going through the leaded glass doors.

Sometimes there were only two houses on the block, sometimes one. Inside, the occupants gathered around long tables in dining rooms whose mantels were taller than the papas, and where the mamas summoned the cooks by tapping a foot on pedals under the tables. Across a long center hallway from the dining room would be a library with books stored so high wheeled steppers were provided to retrieve them.

In the mornings the father sat at one end of the table, dressed in a seersucker ready for the office, reading *The Times-Picayune,* and partaking of a soft boiled egg in a stemmed cup along with buttered toast cut into small triangles.

The Cow-Catcher

At the streetcar's front window a boy could look down at the "cow catcher," a throwback to earlier days. It was a formidable bumper across the front that seemed to gobble up tracks as the car traveled.

It was not unusual for the motorman to whistle during the entire trip. He whistled waltzes or popular tunes. He'd stop whistling to stomp on the floor pedal when a mule-drawn taffy wagon crossed the tracks. Clang, clang, clang. "Darn them mules." Then he might give us a melodious "If I Had a Talking Picture of You."

At one point he would yell, "Oc-taaaaav-ya. Oc-taaaaav-ya next," In an aside he'd say. "That's yours, boy, next."

There were certain courtesies associated with streetcar riding: A boy had to inform the motorman of his destination in "a loud, clear voice," and he had to thank the motorman also in "a loud, clear voice" when he jumped from the folding door.

It was the streetcar that introduced me to my city.

GRANDMAS, FRENCH KNOTS & *CAFE AU LAIT*

Dunking a French bread knot in *cafe au lait* is a basic right in New Orleans. One never neglects the privilege.

I wore long pants before I was aware that people in other cities never had New Orleans French bread, whose flaky crispness results from a series of circumstances having to do with humidity or something. Also I became aware that coffee elsewhere was a different color than ours.

I was impressed by that fact when "in the service" training to save humanity from threatened enslavement. There I learned that the guys in my barracks were accustomed to seeing the bottom of their cup through the coffee. I was stunned when I first saw the bottom of my coffee cup. I would continue seeing the bottom of my coffee cup (and my metal mess pail) until we defeated the enemy and I returned home to delicious tar-black chicory coffee.

Luckiest Kids

Seldom do I think of coffee without thinking of my grandmothers. If you were the first grandchild for both not only were you among the luckiest kids on earth but you got plenty advice. And learned things.

One of mine was a gentle German woman, Ann Estella Frantz, who married a German named Nicholas Schneider. The other was Mary Elia Wright (half English, half Irish) who married a Frenchman named Frank Louis Barrois, for whom I was named.

My paternal grandmother, Grandma, was less than five feet tall. She was frail and with black hair that reached far below her waist. Her daughter Myrtle brushed her hair daily - seven days a week, year after year - and rolled it atop her head where it remained pinned until bedtime. She wore tiny pierced earrings, long dresses, and shuffled in bedroom slippers. She spoke little and with great difficulty, having suf-

fered a stroke when in her 40s.

The huge portrait of her that hung in a gilded frame over a mantel was of a handsome young lady attired in taffeta and lace and with a cameo brooch at her throat. She kept vigils burning and fresh flowers in her Downtown home. Her enjoyment was being with her family and listening to classical music on the Victrola. She marveled that as a small boy I could select her favorites, and wind and operate the machine when standing on a horse hair stuffed ottoman. Every night she knelt at her bed and murmured prayers with closed eyes.

My maternal grandmother, whom I named Mumzie, was just about five feet tall, and had been long widowed and independent when I arrived. She had thin, fine hair that she poked at and puffed up with her fingers as she spoke. She wore heels and stockings until she died at age 97. She kept vigils and fresh flowers in her Uptown home. She advocated positive thinking long before Norman Vincent Peale, and often admonished me: "Don't say can't. There is no such word as can't." She enjoyed reading, and was not enthused over television. Every night she knelt beside her bed and whispered prayers.

Both left me with profound marks and enriched memories, none more lasting than those of having coffee at their homes.

The Agate Pot

At Grandma's the coffee was dripped in a large gray agate pot. After the brewing the pot was placed in a pan of water over a low flame to keep it piping hot. It was served until it was gone. Another pot was brewed in the afternoon. The family and visitors sat around a large round table which always had a platter of pastry.

My young cousin Joyce and I each were served a knot of French bread heavy with butter and a big cup of coffee into which was poured syrupy condensed milk until just the right color, sort of tan.

We dunked the knots into coffee and sucked on them, chewed them, and mopped up their debris in our cups with spoons.

At Mumzie's the coffee was dripped in one of her agate

pots which varied in size to suit the occasion. For two persons she used her tiny two-cupper, a white vessel I have.

When brewing was done she poured the fresh coffee into a sauce pan and heated it with cream. In those days cream rose to the top of the milk bottle just below the cardboard cap. Mumzie insisted milk was never the same after "they homo-gized it."

I explained that in homogenization the cream was evenly distributed in the milk. In a tone of exasperation, she replied: "You believe that?"

My mother dripped coffee daily in a white agate pot, and used electric perkers only when serving many. My wife dripped coffee in a four-cup white agate pot, tediously slow, never hurrying to pour more water, never pouring the brew until the pot was full, and nodding as she waited. I still drip coffee in those old pots.

Often I have a cup, and rip off a French bread knot, smear it with no fat spread and dunk it. I am not alone at the table. They are there, the four lovely ladies in my life.

WHEN NEW ORLEANS NEIGHBORHOODS WERE PORE-INFESTED

At one time New Orleans was a hotbed of "open pores." Our neighborhood was plagued with them. As treacherous as they once appeared to be pores passed into oblivion like nickel Cokes and soda fountains.

My mother talked about my pores incessantly. Through a closed bathroom door I heard her. "Dry yourself good before you come out, and go stand by the heater until your pores close. You hear?"

Pores, I knew at a tender age, were very quiet. They opened and closed without making a sound. I'd rub my arm with a towel and peer at my skin. I knew pores were associated with skin because when I was a toddler my mother rubbed my skin with a towel as she spoke of my pores. We were "drying the pores" to help "close" them. Wet pores, I was certain, could not close. Open pores, God forbid! were an abomination, like dirt behind the ears.

The dear lady could see behind my ears when we were in different rooms. She had instinct about such things. Gingerly I would dab a wet cloth behind my ears, and when I emerged from the bathroom my mother would proclaim: "You didn't wash behind your ears."

"Yes I did."

"Not with soap. You just splashed water behind your ears."

It was scary how she could do that.

For long I thought we were trying to rub off my pores. It was later I discovered we were sealing them. But where were they?

I would look intently at my arm, rub my skin with my fingers trying to spot a pore. Nothing. I'd look in the mirror but not once did I see a pore, not even with a magnifying glass.

How was I to know when my pores closed? I would sit

on my bed, petting Sammy the spitz, waiting for my pores to close before I went outside to play. Sometimes I'd become so engrossed in what I was doing I'd forget I was waiting for my pores to close.

"Are you still in your room? Don't you want to go outside?"

"Oh-uh. Ha. I was waiting for my pores to close and forgot."

"Go ahead. They're closed now."

A Big Mystery

There was no explaining it. My mother could tell when pores were closed without even coming into the room where they were.

Something awesome must have happened when a kid left the house with open pores but I was never sure what. Once my mother said she didn't want me to catch my "death of cold." That did it. For the rest of my life I would never venture outside with open pores. It was suicide!

I noticed that my mother didn't much care if my father's pores were open or shut. Not once did I ever hear her warn him about his open pores. He never stood in front of the heater. He showered, hurriedly dressed and was on his way to work with his pores open! Or did pores wear out with age? Would they close permanently when I got older?

The mystery of pores broadened when I was in the Army protecting the free world from Fascism and overcoming the only fear I had - fear itself. President Franklin Delano Roosevelt had told us that the only fear we had to be concerned about was fear itself. Apparently he'd never heard of pores. It occurred to me that Sara Delano Roosevelt was a delinquent mother.

In the Army barracks not a single man was concerned about his pores. In New Orleans all my friends had them. I distinctly recall one of them yelling to me, "I can't come out yet; my pores ain't closed."

Awake in Forest

As a soldier I lay awake on icy ground in a German forest, clad in long woolies and wrapped in a blanket, wondering about my pores. I survived the war. My Commander-in-Chief Roosevelt was right: there was nothing to fear, not even open pores.

A day after I returned home I was dressed and waited for a friend's car horn to blast. At the sound of it I kissed her on the cheek. "Bye, Mama."

Her eyes were wide with astonishment. "Didn't you shampoo? And you're going out already?!"

MAKING DO-DO (doh-doh) - DELIGHTFUL, PERVERSE CUSTOM

For generations the young Orleanian made do-do, another French influence.

Most New Orleans kids under 12 took a nap in the afternoons. Our mamas insisted. Come rain, shine, thunder, hell, high water or death in the family do-do was a must.

In early afternoon a pall fell over our neighborhood. There was no arguing. It was afternoon and time for a nap. I would insist that I wasn't tired. The reply was instant: "Take off your shoes. And those socks. Pee-u!"

In the middle of an exciting game of mumbletypeg when one kid had a third of his face buried in mud under a camphor tree trying to retrieve a sliver of wood with his teeth - it was sheer joy - do-do time was announced. "Come in NOW."

We didn't escape do-do even when vacationing. During long hot summer afternoons in Covington, my cousins and I would venture off beyond a wooded area. But we heard the call as clearly as though they used a bullhorn. "Nap timmmme."

We'd ignore the call until it was delivered with a threat. "No movie tonight." Nighttime in the Covington woods with no prospect of seeing a movie was, in today's vernacular, the worst possible scenario. We called it "a fine fix."

We'd march inside, lie across our beds with teeth clenched, lips in pouts and determined not to sleep one wink. More often than not we fell into a torpor, sometimes until the sun faded and it was too late for having fun outdoors.

There were moments, however, when halfway between being out of it and with it, somewhere at the edge of euphoria, all seemed well.

Before long I was a father of three wide-eyed children.

My wife, herself a do-do child, insisted they rest. "You don't have to sleep, just lie there quietly. Don't speak."

After three minutes of silence a whispering voice would call out, "Mama, is it time to wake up yet?"

"Not yet."

The more resistant they became the more persistent were we. Like their father and mother before them they succumbed. The poor dears never knew what hit them.

Before long, two grandchildren were at our house spending the day - two boys under age four with motors inside them. They liked to walk and run. Their principal attribute was motion.

"What time do they take their nap?" I asked.

"Ah-ha-ha-ho-ha, Daddy," Sally Ann laughed. Napping was no longer mandatory, she said, but should they topple over while playing we could carry them to "a sofa or something."

They never toppled over. I toppled over.

When I mentioned that they should "make do-do," they smiled wickedly. Do-do sounded like wild fun.

I placed them on a couch, covered them with an Afghan, pulled the drapes, stretched out in a lounger and closed my eyes.

There was a whisper, "Pop-pop."

"Shhh. I'm right here. Be quiet."

There was a moment of silence, then, "Pop-pop."

"Shhhh, don't awaken your brother."

"He not sleep-in. He laugh-in."

"Shhhh. Do-do time."

Into Dreamland

I closed my eyes, and the boy was quiet. It was as if I were back in childhood, first day-dreaming, then slipping into a stupor.

When I regained consciousness I popped open one eye

and saw the Afghan on my legs. The sofa was empty. "Nicholas? Christopher?"

"They're in here with me," Happy called out.

I went into the kitchen where my wife was stirring a pot of fudge on the stove. The boys were standing on a chair looking on intently.

"What are you doing?" I asked.

Nicholas' eyes widened. "Cook," he exclaimed.

"Cook," Christopher echoed.

Until Nicholas was seven and Christopher six I attempted to get them to make do-do. I rocked them, danced around the rooms with them, spun them round and round like a top.

Nothing worked.

It saddens me to think that my grandsons grew up in New Orleans without making do-do. That's what happens with a discerning generation that can discern before their mothers take them home from the hospital.

THE LONG TREK FROM AGE OF INNOCENCE TO THE NEW AGE

Every neighborhood had a "show." We never called it theater. The show was the second most revered landmark in our neighborhood right after the church. Or was it right before the church?

Ours was a three-block walk from our houses over an aging wooden bridge that crossed Bayou St. John at Dumaine Street. We walked on the streetcar tracks in the center of the bridge, balancing steps with extended arms, each betting the others we could walk full length without falling.

The show was named Imperial, a misnomer for so plain a place. It was situated in the center of a row of double cottages on N. Hagan, and with its box office smack on the sidewalk just feet from neighbors' stoops and a tiny alley away from their bedrooms. There was no center aisle inside, but two side ones, one of which led to the rest rooms where doors were sprung open and slammed shut continuously.

The Imperial was not only our entertainment center but a source of knowledge. We were there much more often than the library.

Bank Night

In the 30s the likes of Hollywood's Stepin Fetchit and local radio personality Henry Dupre appeared on its stage, but I recall the stage being used mostly on Bank Night when vast sums of money, sometimes as much as $300, were awarded to some lucky person in attendance. The night when the pot was at a stupendous $600 the management placed loudspeakers outside so ticket holders lined up on the *banquettes* could hear the goings on.

When we would hoot and holler a giant who passed himself off as the usher flashed a light in our faces and yelled,

"You boys in there. Quiet!" His name was Oliver Himbert, but we referred to him as The Giant and regarded him as a bouncer. When adults we would learn of Himbert's connection to the Imperial's most famous patron. Himbert's sister-in-law had a little girl named Dorothy and was married to a man named Lambour. Dorothy and Oliver Himbert's young sister frequently went to the Imperial together until Dorothy won the Miss New Orleans competition. Then, she left town and didn't return to the Imperial until 1936 when she appeared on its screen as "The Jungle Princess." And she had dropped the "b" in Lambour.

The show's summertime ventilation was provided by wooden transoms on the side walls just below the ceiling. They were opened and closed with ropes manipulated by Himbert. The show's mechanical ventilation was provided by a fan taller than any of us. It blew high velocity winds from the stage area smack into our faces. Wind whistled in our ears as they flapped. Our eyes teared.

Plank Benches

We sat in the first five rows of plank benches. Conventional theater seats behind the benches were for adults. Many a summer night we came home wheezing and sniffling after being out in that wind for two or more hours. Walking home balanced on the trolley tracks we could hear the Imperial's wind roaring in our skulls.

The Imperial was built in 1922 by our neighbor, the senior Rene Brunet, a tall, fastidiously attired gentleman. Each strand of his full head of wavy silver hair remained in place in all seasons, appearing remarkably like that of the matinee idols we saw on the Imperial's screen.

On Sundays we arrived at the show at 2 p.m., still burping from mashed potatoes and fried chicken, and came out at about 7 p.m. after having seen the comedy, cartoon and newsreel twice and the feature once and a half. We'd spend exactly 20 cents, 10 for the show, five for an orange drink and five for a Hershey bar.

Frequently the feature film was advertised as "a romance." There was nothing funnier than watching Kay Francis in those romantic films.

Either she was lavishly dressed with ermine collars that covered her ears, hats whose plumes cascaded down her back and gowns whose decolletage plunged to her belly button, or she was running around in her teddies, stockings and high-heel satin slippers.

However dressed she always held a cigarette in a long silver holder when talking with George Brent, always impeccably groomed in black tie, and with glistening black, pomaded hair. Kay would toss back her head, laugh in a husky voice and blow smoke rings in Brent's face.

Kay Blew Smoke

Kay had a talent for fluttering her eyelids as she blew smoke at those she hardly knew. Usually she was married but not to George who was always with her. Her husband was at the bank. He was president. He looked like her grandfather.

With her left hand she held a cigarette and with her right a martini with a tiny olive in an elegant long stem glass. She'd take a sip and a puff and laugh. "Darling", Brent would coo. When she fluttered her eyelashes her eyebrows leapt into a big arch near her hairline.

Carefree as she seemed, Kay always stopped short of visibly breaching any commandments, as far as we could tell. Though it seemed extremely naughty that George Brent would be in the same room with her as she sat before a mirror adjusting her brassiere straps, she was, after all, a movie star. We knew that Hollywood people did all sorts of things that our mothers and aunts and even our neighbors didn't do. For instance, movie stars got divorced! And they walked around in their teddies.

All except Norma Shearer. She was my Beautiful Goddess. She smoked, but adjusted her brassiere straps off camera.

Once I saw her remove her stockings in the presence of Franchot Tone, but I forgave her because I knew she had seen too many Kay Francis movies.

In recent years I was stunned to learn in her biography that Norma, when widowed, entertained just-made-16 Mickey Rooney in her MGM dressing room. His mother complained to the studio boss that Norma was corrupting her little boy. Later, Norma was pictured dancing at the Coconut Grove with George Raft. She preferred short people.

We were not aware of celebrity haughtiness. Hollywood kept secrets.

There are no secrets now. Even if you don't want to know someone's secrets they tell you anyway. You could plead, "Shut up, I don't want to hear your secrets." But they're on television telling all. Mothers tell on daughters and daughters on fathers and teachers on students and students on principals and little old ladies tell on little old men.

Our culture demands we know everything. The pregnant 16-year-old insists that the whole world know who the father is. At one time that was the best kept neighborhood secret. In those days had a 16-year-old girl found herself "in that way" she would have disappeared in the dark of night during the Christmas holidays. Vanished!

'Where is Eulola?'

If you'd have asked, "Where is Eulola?" Her own mother might have replied, "Eulola who?"

The following spring Eulola might return to tell neighbors she had visited her Aunt Weezy Mae in Arkansas and was having such fun she forgot to come back. The incident was never broadcast and *The Times-Picayune* did not interview the wretch.

Now a pregnant seventh grader doesn't go to Arkansas. She goes directly to a neighborhood clinic, then to a TV talk show to unburden the pain of living with her secret.

On such shows she reveals the name of the father, who also appears alongside his wife and three children who have forgiven him so that he will not be shackled for the rest of his life with such a secret. Also present are lawyers, a psychologist and social worker who urge all to unload guilt immediately. Viewers may call an 800 number to order a video account of the misery for only $19.95.

The old neighborhood show will never return, nor will Kay Francis and the Age of Innocence. Norma Shearer, alone and still elegant when withering in a wheel chair in a California hills rest home, kept her secrets to the end.

She was a lady, Norma was. Almost.

WHEN THEY MADE CLABBER UNDER THE SINK

Without closing my eyes I can see them under the kitchen sink, those glass milk bottles whose contents appeared lumpier as each day passed. They told me it was clabber.

Much later in life I would discover that clabber was, indeed, putrefied milk, more politely called curdled, and was the first step in creating Creole Cream Cheese. In the 20s and 30s hardly a household in New Orleans was without clabber in the process.

I watched my mother and Teen, a frail tall woman who always wore pinch nose spectacles and a flowered dress protected by a starched white apron, as they poured small amounts of leftover milk into those bottles under the sink. They would hold up a bottle from time to time to observe it and make comments.

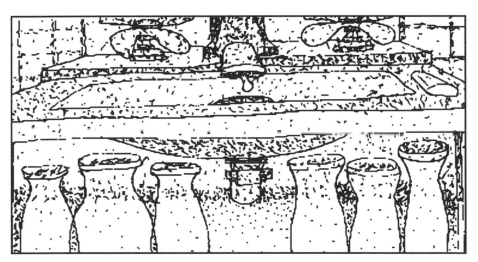

The bottles would stand there for days pent up with gases and foul odor, I was certain of it. At the proper time (there were those who knew when) Teen would exclaim: "Miss Mae, Ah think our clabba's jus' 'bout ripe, nah." The lumpy, sour mass would be poured into a gauzy cloth that they squeezed in their hands. It wasn't easy to watch. The revolting residue was left out overnight. The next day the clabbered remain was whipped, molded and chilled. All of the procedure was carried out with great enthusiasm by Teen and my mother. They made it seem a joyful task.

Just before eating the white blob they topped it with sweet cream and sprinkled sugar on it. They sat at the kitchen table with raptured expressions while spooning it into their mouths.

Not once did they persuade me to "taste it, just once." Not even by force. Just seeing clabber was enough to shake a boy of five.

Few Orleanians today savor the sport of making their own Creole Cream Cheese, a tedious chore that requires time and special utensils. I know of only one. Mickey O'Dwyer carries on the tradition, and can describe the process with that same bubbly glow that animated the faces of my mother and Teen many years ago. He might be the only one in town with clabber under roof.

I was not able to taste the magnificent treat called Creole Cream Cheese until I was a much wiser person, an adult.

NATURE'S WRATH RECALLED AS FIRST CLASS FRIGHT

My first recollection of pure fright came as a fifth grader when I saw a tornado whirl along the neutral ground on Franklin Avenue.

At the time it appeared that a sizeable portion of my family would be blown en masse to their eternal reward. I would not become a sixth grader after all.

We sat around a big round table, adults discussing Huey Long as they customarily did, and my cousin Joyce and I dunking French bread knots in *cafe au lait* as we customarily did when visiting Grandma and Papa, my paternal grandparents.

When the wind whipped the tablecloth into rumples and blew away daisy petals from the vase on the table, Aunt Myrt pulled down the windows. The conversation grew louder to overcome the howls of intensifying winds.

We heard my mother's piercing cry from the front parlor. "Come see. Garbage cans are rolling in the street. There's a tree branch flying by. And ..... a mailbox! Come see. It's getting worse.

The adults rushed from the table. Joyce and I remained to attack jelly rolls.

Get the Ferns

We heard them shouting commands. "Harold, take in the ferns." "Frank, unhook the swing." "Pull up the awning." Finally, someone shouted, "The children. Somebody get the children."

We were already on our way to the front of the house, leaving behind a platter of belly fillers. In the hall we could feel the sting of winds and hear its hissing sounds as it swept through the house from the open front door.

"Ohhhh. Look." From the sidelights looking beyond the porch we saw a section of streetcar tracks rise from their grassy bed then drop again like an ocean wave.

My father, uncle and grandfather pressed against the door unable to close it entirely. My mother and aunt joined them. My grandmother looked on from a room away, murmuring, "Mercy, mercy."

The wind popped shades from lamps and whipped curtains into ghostly forms that hovered near the ceiling.

When the door closed the men pushed furniture against it. "Not the piano," my aunt yelled to them. "It's just been tuned."

The women took us to a bedroom where my mother and aunt dropped to their knees before a vigil light at a statue. Grandma was seated on the edge of a bed, mumbling, "Mercy, mercy." Their eyes were closed. My cousin and I were wide-eyed.

We heard things smashing against the house and saw fencing parts sailing past the windows. The shutters shook and rattled. We seemed to tremble with the house. It was the scariest day of my life. They told us, "We must have seen a tornado."

Dazed & Draped

We drove home through rubble and saw dead pets in the streets. People stood on the *banquettes* dazed. Some sobbed. Later we learned that Uncle Frank and other neighbors rescued a terrified woman who was draped with a towel and stood in a bathtub surrounded by rubble.

That was my only experience with a tornado, but I was to become proficient in hurricane survival.

In those days hurricanes were nameless "storms". At some point the storms were called hurricanes and baptized with females names that were popular at the time such as Agnes, Beulah and Cora. We were not aware that meteorology was an occupation.

Growing up all we knew about a hurricane was that

when one was coming the family packed dog, candles, kerosene lamps, blankets, change of underwear (in case of an emergency) and rosaries and left for my maternal grandmother's house where it was "safe Uptown." Mumzie's house was nearly 100 years old, built like a fortress with thick shutters and a sturdy front door that would resist the most persistant winds.

True, the chimneys collapsed sometimes, and trees disappeared, but the house stood firm.

We assembled there with four generations of family members, sometimes as many as 25 of us including a few of Mumzie's neighbors who were "afraid to be alone."

We'd sip port, eat sandwiches and petit fours by candlelight, and respond to Mumzie's Litany of the Saints. And lived to tell of it.

Later, married and blessed with children to protect, I continued hurrying to Mumzie's sturdy old house with my family, flashlight, blankets, rosaries and dachshund.

BEST TEACHERS HAD EYES BEHIND HEADS

At Our Lady of the Holy Rosary school in the old neighborhood sixth and seventh grade boys attended classes in a weathered Creole cottage on Esplanade Avenue. That was in 1935.

The two-room house had white porcelain knobs on its doors, splintered wooden plank floors, walls and ceilings, and windows that rattled in the wind. Up front near the teacher was a pot belly iron stove with sooty black stack that rose to pierce a tin roof. When it rained the splattered roof made such a racket we couldn't hear what the nun was saying.

On cold days Sister Ann Marie fed the old stove with chunks of wood. We kept our sweaters and coats on, and she wrapped herself in a big black woolen shawl. We clapped our feet together and blew warm breaths into our hands. On hot days we sweat a lot. The nun dabbed her brow dry with a big white handkerchief.

In such an atmosphere we learned certain truths. The first was that we enthusiastically embrace without question all that was taught, and to come away each day more learned than the day before. Or else. The teacher was always right, as were the parents at home. Also always right were the priests in the pulpit and all adults in the neighborhood.

Her Back To Us

A saying of the day was that some teachers had eyes in the backs of their heads. Sister Ann Marie was the most baffling of all. The nun would be at the blackboard with her back to us and her right arm high above her head with chalk in hand "working out an equation."

Before she began to "solve the problem," she stated firmly: "No one is to take his eyes off the board as I write. No one is to look in a book. No one is to turn around." As she wrote speedily, she added, "No one is to copy this. No one is to ... Mr. Leopold, why are you tapping that ruler?"

"Not me, sistah," said Leopold, dropping the ruler.

"It was you, Mr. Leopold, I saw you," she said, never turning around and continuing to fill the board with numerals.

We all saw him. But how did she see him?

She was a St. Joseph nun who lived in a convent not far away on Ursulines Avenue. The sisters there were enveloped in black wool from neck to ankle, and with gigantic starched white bibs and headpieces of white starched panels overlaid with black veils that extended below their waists. And she had seen Leopold!

Long before we reached her "room" we had heard about her ability to see things that were behind her. "She has eyes in the back of her head," experienced pupils warned us. We were called pupils, not students.

Ink Splashes

She never knew much about girls. Girls were in another building and played in an area separated from ours by a high board fence. She knew about boys. She knew when a boy chewed gum even when he never moved his jaw. She knew when a boy had his book open on page 42 when she had commanded that he open it on page 17.

For some assignments we used pens that were dipped into glass "ink wells" depressed in the desk top. She knew when a boy splashed ink on his desk when she had ordered us not to use ink for the assignment.

"You splashed ink on your desk, Mr. Duhe?"

Duhe's face was fire red.

"You think that's funny, Mr. Leopold?"

"No sistah."

"Come up here, Mr. Leopold, and write the answer to this problem."

Before he began to write, Sister folded her arms with

hands hidden in the great black sleeves, stepped out onto the porch of the old house and looked out at St. Louis Cemetery No. 3 on Esplanade Avenue

Leopold Frantic

Leopold was frantic, urging anyone to give him the answer. He was demanding the answer, threatening with a clenched fist and the eraser which he held over his head in wind up position.

Servat held up a piece of paper with the answer, and Leopold wrote it on the blackboard.

"Ah'm finished, sistah."

"Finished are you? Already?"

"Yeah."

She came into the room, patting perspiration from her face with a big white handkerchief. "Mr. Pfister, stop scratching your head."

She went to Servat's desk, looked at the page he had held up, erased one of the numerals and corrected it with another. She held it up for Leopold to see. "Is this your answer, Mr. Leopold?"

"No, sistah", he said with head hanging. Then, smiling, he looked up and said, "But I was close, huh?"

Sister Ann Marie squinched her eyes and bowed her head. She shook with laughter.

We all laughed aloud.

Minutes later we sat outside on discarded church pews in a tin-roofed shed to have our "baloney" and pickle sandwiches, busily swatting at buzzing flies as we ate. After lunch we stood with heads bowed in circles around the nun as she listened to us recite the Grace After Meals.

Afterwards, we ran wild in the dusty yard, screaming and tumbling. Sometimes Sister would toss up a ball and swing at it with a bat so hard that the long rosary hanging from her waist wrapped around her skirt. Like Babe Ruth, she'd yell,

"It's going to go way over there by the fence. Get back, Mr. Canepa." And then she'd whop another over our heads, over the dilapidated gate that opened to the avenue.

Soon we were back in the cottage, sweaty and panting, standing by our desks saying a short prayer before the beginning of a history lesson. Now solemn, the nun was at the blackboard, her back to us. "Turn around, Mr. Schneider. I'm going to be asking you a question."

I learned from her.

'AMO, AMAS, AMAT ... YOU FOOLISH KEED'

In high school we encountered Father William A. Fillinger, S.J. He was at the Jesuit school a 12-block walk or a short bike ride from home.

It seemed cruel that 12-year-olds should be exposed to the man, but the Jesuits fancied themselves as knowing best. Their logic was that if a student survived nine months with this man he could hurdle all academic barricades. We did not pursue our studies Ad Majorem Dei Gloriam (To the Greater Glory of God) as the Jesuits would have had it, but rather to keep Father Fillinger as calm as we were able.

I remember the man as if he were a brand burnt into my psyche. He was unforgettable from the top of his cherubic head to the tips of his shabby shoes. The cheeks were rosy and delicately streaked with veins. The sparse wiry white hair stood straight up on the skull. The bushy eyebrows arched rimless glasses that he looked over, seldom through. The ice blue eyes sparkled. The teeth were heavily stained with nicotine, gnarled, and with generous spaces between them. The large round head rested upon broad shoulders without visible assistance of a neck.

The torso was stocky with an abundant middle that forced his black cassock's broad sash to the groin. The shoes were severely scuffed and the white socks were fully exposed below the frock's ragged hem.

Awesome Wisdom

The man's wisdom was awesome, his recall astounding. Again and again he reminded us that he was a friend of Father Yenni who wrote our textbook, New Yenni Latin Grammar, copyright 1920. He often quoted entire pages, paragraphs and page numbers without referring to the book.

In winsome moments he related brief tales of his personal life. Once he ripped open his cassock and lifted a wool undershirt to reveal a plump chest. It was foliated with wiry white hairs looking much like those on his head, and spanning it was a tattoo likeness of the ship on which he served in the Norwegian Navy.

His accent was heavy, and when agitated he spewed saliva in rapid streams repeatedly, shouting phrases to emphasize diction. When he shouted "Errando discimus, errando discimus, errando discimus" it was best not to be close to him.

Errando discimus, we learned, meant, "we learn by mistakes," a fact the priest never considered when we made one, which was frequently.

A roomful of adolescents sweated with anxiety and fear that the man might point a stubby finger at them in search of an answer. Some went through the Latin hour unable to speak without studdering. As a result we became sophomores knowing more Latin than English.

We knew that *habitat in urbe* means "he lives in the city" without the vaguest idea what an isosceles triangle is. When the first semester ended our Civic books were like new, our Latin grammars frayed and stained.

Many men in New Orleans might not remember their wedding anniversary date, or that their brake tags expired but they know that *amo, amas, amat* means "I love, you love, he (she, it) loves." Some remember the page number in their Yenni book. It's Page 58. Father Fillinger told us that the verb "to love" was basic for understanding the course. Pages 58 and 59 in my book are barely visible from learning "to love". The only practical application we found for taking Latin was that we could stealthilty tack signs on the backs of girls that spelled out "Amo te" (I love you). They never knew what it meant. It drove them crazy.

One morning Father Fillinger pointed a stubby, tobacco-stained finger at me, called my name and requested the conjugation of the imperfect tense of *amo*, I love.

A Face Glowed

The proper response was amabam pronounced amAbam. I swallowed and it came out, "amaBAM," My face glowed with warmth.

The priest came within two feet of me with a breath that reeked of stale tobacco, and said, "Say dot again. I dint hear dot too gut."

"AmaBAM," I repeated. Perspiration dripped down both legs.

"No," he shouted, "amAbam, vit dee ax-hent on dee AH. Tell me it again."

"AmaBAM," I said, nearly collapsing.

'AmAAAAAAAbam," he shouted. Sit down."

He pointed to another student. "Tell Mr. Schneider how to say it."

The boy stood, shaking, and blundered, "AmaBUM."

"You a bum. Sit down, bum. Who can say it right?"

One of the freshmen football players stood up, cleared his throat and stated loudly, "Amabo."

"You ban sleeping, you foolish foo-ball player. Sumbuddy kick you in dee head? Dots not even vot vee doing. Sit down, ox."

The priest clasped his hands behind his head and walked swiftly in and out of the rows of desks. "AmAbam, AmAbam, AmAAAAAAAAAbam", he wailed.

"Effer-ree-buddy loook un dee boook at dee verd und vee say all togedder - AmAbam, amAbam, amAbam."

We said it along with him, over and over.

He was in front of me, pointing a stubby finger, and grinning, flashing brown teeth and gaps. "You say it for me, Mr. Schneider, all by yurself."

A Triple Offense

I stood. "AmaBAM." I could not believe I said it wrong again. I spurted, nervously, "AmaBAM, amaBAM, amaBAM" tripling the offense.

Father Fillinger spun around with hands covering his ears. "Stop saying dot, ofer and ofer, fool."

There was nervous giggling.

The priest looked at me, his brow in a deeply creased frown. "You making fun uf me, Mr. Schneider?"

"Ohhhh, no, no, no Father." My hands were on my desk in a puddle of sweat.

"Den, now you say it right. Tink. Just tink. Und you say it."

I opened my mouth and it came out - "amAbam." A chill bolted from my nape to my behind.

Father Fillinger showed all of his dental gaps in a broad smile, approached me, patted my head with a hand of stubby fingers, and said, "You see how eesy ven you pay atten-shun? Dot vas gut. You neffer, neffer forget now. Not Neffer."

OUR BACKYARD WAS HUGE, PEACEFUL PARADISE

We grew up and old without giving much thought to the blessing that our neighborhood's backyard was City Park. As youngsters we visited there on skates, bikes or walked barefooted in the summertime.

We were unaware that it was steep with history and romance and its early ownership linked to both wealth and poverty.

Initial owner of the undeveloped acreage was Francois Hery who came into possession of it soon after the city was founded. When he died his farmland went to Santiago Lorreins, whose daughter Francoise inherited his plantation. It would be known from then on as "the Allard plantation" named for Francoise's husband, Jean Louis Allard. He built an imposing two-story house facing Bayou St. John at a point close to where City Park Avenue approaches the bayou today. Allard's heir, Louis Jr., mortgaged the property then lost it. John McDonogh acquired it. His fortune was willed to the public school systems of New Orleans and Boston, and included the Allard property. The old man desired that the city lease the land to farmers, so that in later years it could be sold off as suburban lots with the city receiving profits. But after McDonogh's death his will would not be honored. One newspaper suggested that the city drain the soggy land and use it for amusements. The city liked the idea, but first there had to be a law suit. By 1857 the new park was open.

Fantasy Land

We knew none of that. The park was Fantasy Land. There were fields and lanes, forests, giant trees, pools and lagoons. A kid could be zapped a zillion miles to another land. His skiff floated through rippling passageways arched with blooming tropicals and hanging vines. Pirates might have been around a bend. With a crude pole and bent pin to pierce a slimy worm's innards a kid might catch a sun perch, or a hunk of moss caught on a floating twig. Under mighty oaks a kid could shoot a bird there with a BB gun. Then cry. Then bury it.

At the big pool we lost our breaths tumbling from the tip of the Hell Diver again and again until our ears buzzed and eyes burned. We could climb and jump screaming from Suicide Oak. Under Dueling Oak we fought with cane spears, toppling over into piles - all dead. At the Peristyle we skated round and round, then mounted great cement lions to lick ice cream cones. From broad concrete steps we wiggled dusty toes in a lagoon.

On rainy days we visited the quiet tomb-like museum with its statues of naked people and paintings as big as our bed matresses. Ancient weapons, arrow heads, lacy fans and pottery were locked in glass cases.

The Big Casino had everything a sweaty boy needed - whirling ceiling fans, sodas, peanuts, popcorn, snowballs. At an Iron Claw machine a dexterous kid might snatch a dazzling gift for his mama, maybe a corkscrew with a picture of Rin Tin Tin on it.

FDR, RWL & RSM

We saw history being made at City Park. President Franklin D. Roosevelt, Governor Richard W. Leche and Mayor Robert S. Maestri shared the back seat in FDR's shiny new touring car that was shipped to New Orleans for the dedication of Roosevelt Mall in the park.

We arrived early at the mall, freshly paved by the WPA (Works Progress Administration) and lined with skinny young oak trees. We dropped our bikes far from the sidewalk and stood in the street waiting for the president. That day I learned something was wrong with the president. He never stood.

He spoke to us through a big microphone that blotted out half of his face. The other half was blotted out by a little kid in short white pants and shoes and socks, as though he were making his communion. He stood on the running board holding onto the door of the car, and with his face smack in the president's. It was Paul Montreuil, a neighborhood kid whose daddy was park superintendent.

We were on the front row just a few feet from the president. After a few forgettable words from FDR, the boy was removed from the running board and we went home for lunch. I had "baloney" on French and an Orphan Annie chocolate shake. FDR, RWL and RSM were whisked to Antoine's for an historic meal including "ershtas Rocka-fellah", according to RSM.

A few years later we watched history in the park again. The lasting memory is of a domed altar with nine-foot crucifix set at one end of the stadium for the Eucharistic Congress. His Eminence from Chicago and our local and long-winded Archbishop Francis Rummel were there. FDR spoke over the radio to us because he was too busy to visit. In the evening 70,000 attended Mass there, each holding a lighted candle.

Kites & Soccer

Sometimes on Saturdays my Dad and I flew kites and licked chocolate cones in the park. On Sunday afternoons we sat on a grassy stretch by the tennis courts to watch a soccer match. Sometimes the players came sliding and tumbling within inches of us. We'd sit in the skimpy shade of young palm trees for hours watching men bang heads together and skin their behinds sliding on the turf. Often we actually heard the sound of a body smashing a body and the accompanying agonizing groans. Some players were so ragged by game's end they were carried from the field. On one occasion an ambulance was summoned.

At age 10 I learned that soccer was a foreign game. No

player spoke English. It was amazing that all those men would travel so far from home to come to City Park behind the tennis courts to play for nothing. There were no trophies for the victors. Most of the time it was difficult to tell who were the victors because there was no score board and all of the players appeared beaten. Their only reward was weak applause from the 20 or so onlookers sprawled out on the lawn or seated on wooden boxes.

Usually the adversaries were Germans and South Americans, or so they sounded. After a kid attended a number of these matches he could pick up a few German and Spanish expressions. *Dummkoff* and *estupido* come to mind.

If more than a handful of players collapsed on the field there'd be an extended time out. During this period we walked to the Big Casino for an ice cream cone. When we returned to our spot under a palm tree the referee blew a whistle, players sprung to their feet, groaned, and the game resumed.

First Date

At a certain age, when my Dad stopped going regularly to the fracas by the tennis courts, I asked a neighborhood girl to accompany me. I considered it my first date. We walked to the grassy space by the tennis courts.

She was visibly shaken when she saw that there were no grandstands. "Where do we sit?" she asked. "Wherever we want," I answered.

We watched soccer for 10 minutes, and were in the Big Casino and a skiff for 2 hours. We had to leave the game because she said she was going to "throw up." She also complained of "crawly things" on her legs. A few years later I took her to her high school prom. The music was too loud, she said.

On Sunday afternoons the Big Casino was filled with parents and whoever else were corralled to watch their Dolly

Dimples perform her spectacular toe dance taught at Miss Zodarinos' School of the Dance and Acrobatics, or some such place. Long before the musicians appeared all of the benches that fanned out from the imposing band stand were occupied.

Excitement was high when the conductor raised his baton to signal a rousing Star Spangled Banner that could be heard across Bayou St. John. For the National Anthem everyone stood with hundreds of hands across as many chests, and all voices sang, sort of.

Four or five of us scooted up a giant oak close to the lagoon for loge seats. We slouched in the cradle of huge branches or straddled them.

The master of ceremonies announced the acts, such as a brother and sister team - Isodilla and Ralphie. She sang and he played the accordion.

Next would be Gloria who sang and Lloyd who played the accordion. Following was Janie and Leo executing an adagio. Their Uncle Theos played the accordion.

Occasionally a performer stomped offstage pouting or in tears after a series of blunders. We'd laugh so hard we'd nearly fall from the tree.

Wrapped in Tulle

At one performance a small girl wrapped in tulle and glittering sequins spun round and round like a top, twirling furiously until she fell into the arms of a man who rushed to the edge of the stage to catch her.

The man carried her away, both of them sobbing. They received more applause than anyone.

We watched another little girl wrapped in tulle and glittering with sequins sing "Frankie and Johnny" to piano accompaniment. She was hootching and kootching and wriggling wildly when one of the ducks in the lagoon joined in with quack blasts, not stopping until she did. The poor dear was inconsolable.

Among the acts were dancers who couldn't, singers who shouldn't have and magicians who weren't. But it was free. And they let us sit in the tree.

To Rest Rooms

During intermission a political figure would make a speech and introduce other politicians and dozens of men and women who "made all of this possible." All said a "few words." At such intervals the audience retreated in a body to rest rooms. The politicians continued handing out certificates, dropping names and patting backs as if an audience were present.

There were always one or two performers done up to appear as Shirley Temple, whose mothers told them a talent scout might be in the audience. They looked nothing like Shirley Temple, but their mothers thought so and they thought so. They wore puffed up skirts and patent leather tap shoes and their head ringlets bounced as they jigged.

Before sunset we had seen dozens of performers flipping, flopping, splitting and rolling in cartwheels. It ended soon after whole families departed or if several tiny performers who appeared early in the program began tossing themselves on the ground in tantrums.

At dusk the "bubble gum man" walked through the crowd. "Bubble gum, here. Gitcha bubble gum."

Men moved a silver screen to the stage, not as big as the one in our neighborhood show but big enough to see a silent Laurel and Hardy, Harold Lloyd and Betty Boop. We laughed and blew bubble gum until our jaws ached.

When the men took away the screen we'd slide down the tree, walk across the stone bridge over the lagoon and through the park and along City Park Avenue to Carrollton and then to Taft Place and Wilson Drive.

"Nite, Tic. Nite Brother. See ya tomorrow."

"Yeah, nite."

Popp's Fountain

Seven years later at Popp's Fountain in City Park, the teenager there with me became someone special. She had brought along a small radio, and sparkling hazel eyes, alluring dimples, scented auburn hair and a winsome smile. We danced slowy around the reflecting pool passing trellises of wisteria as Sinatra sang "All the Things You Are." Five years later we were married.

We returned there often. And with a radio.

IS THAT A GREAT LAKE, OR WHAT?

It is 24 miles wide, 40 miles long, shallow and offers distinguished visual pleasure in an area of undistinguished sameness. Experts tell us that one of those interglacial periods about 70,000,000 years ago is responsible for Lake Pontchartrain's early formation. Some authorities insist it is not a lake (defined as an inland water body) but an extension of the Gulf of Mexico.

Exactly what the big waterhole is does not concern the New Orleanian who cares more that its dark green water burps white caps that sometimes ripple, sometimes churn under a canopy of blue sky that is decorated with sunrays and floating clouds by day and a shining moon and flickering stars by night.

Whatever it is it's the city's backyard, a playground, a source of great delight, and sometimes worry. Sometimes the waters are whipped by menacing winds that threaten residents.

In the 1920s it became obvious that lake waters and storm tides had to be contained to protect expanding development. Instead of raising the levees already constructed, the Orleans Levee Board built a broad and high soil embankment, a super barrier from West End to the industrial Canal. This is held in place by a metal retaining wall driven below the lake surface. Oldtimers say a farsighted Bienville was responsible for New Orleans being where it is, but innovative engineers are responsible for keeping it where he put it.

City dwellers have been going "across the lake" for centuries, since New Orleans' earliest days. Then, fine folk took small craft to the venerable communities of Mandeville and Lewisburg on the lake's north shore. Two hundred years later the north shore remains a popular respite, though expansion has agitated silent woodlands and isolated beaches.

Families packed children and pets, cranked the car and drove to their summer "places." They went to Covington where thick shade was everywhere and trees were heavy with moss. Or they traveled to the Mississippi Gulf Coast, the old Creoles' favorite spot, where long, high wooden piers carried them over shallow gulf waters that were warmed by sun and cooled by breezes.

The men commuted to and from their offices on weekdays. The women and children remained in cottages that were provided with ample screened space, or in rambling two-story houses whose broad verandas offered the comforts of swings and rockers where city folk could "catch the breezes."

Others rented motel cabins that advertised, "Hot and cold running water. Beach towels and umbrellas for rent."

Gravel & Clay

The trip "across the lake" was a challenge for adults, children and pets alike. Roads of gravel and clay could be muddy, dusty, rocky or slick depending on a variety of circumstances that could change from one moment to the next. Road shoulders were considered dangerous. Backseat informants often announced, "Watch the shoulder here. It's tricky."

Families became acquainted with a new malady - "car sickness." Many a bewildered cow watched queasy passengers standing alongside a gravel road getting "car sick."

Orleanians still maintain houses across the lake, but many are permanent residents nowadays. They travel "across the lake" to New Orleans to visit family and friends. They commute to offices and schools speedily passing repetitive sameness along concrete spans.

The screened porches of their homes have been enclosed as "extra rooms" where glass walls protect the household from breezes and other outside annoyances. "Country houses" are air conditioned.

There are no cabins. The townspeople don't swim in rivers now. Everybody has a pool or belongs to the neighborhood "country club" or fitness center.

Covington's Chills

I recall when Covington was a picture-card town whose Main Street courthouse at the square was an oak-shaded gathering spot. City kids rushed to white sand and chilled river water (it could turn them blue) that was hugged by clay bluffs. The river turned and twisted out of sight in rapid current rushing lakeward. All the way to Lake Pontchartrain sunshine shone in streaks through stately pines, wild magnolias and oaks webbed with flowering vines.

In Covington a city kid had a set of local friends he saw daily during the year's hot months. There, where a single signal light hung over one intersection and few STOP signs were necessary, a city kid learned to drive the family car.

He discovered there was a difference in towns' appearances but not their people. City folk and small town folk were much alike, but summertime country life was calmer and cooler.

It was in Covington, at Jim's Beach alongside the Bogafalaya River that emptied into the lake, that I encountered my most sobering childhood incident. Four of us had swum beyond where we were allowed to venture, and when struggling to grasp the small, steep bit of bluff on the opposite side of the river I went under, far under. Then under again and again, way over my head to bottomless depths. I was aware of having gone under the fabled three times and swallowing water. On the fourth time under, when close to panic, my feet felt something solid that seemed to spring me above the water. It was as though I popped up. I reached shore, calmly. We returned to the other side as though nothing happened.

I related the strange happening to no one. If it had happened in these times I could have told people it was my Guardian Angel who popped me out of the water. I would be in videos relating my experience. As it happens nobody knows what really occurred that day beyond Jim's Beach. Except me. And him.

From boyhood to fatherhood there was Nana's summer house in the "woods" and Kettye Malone's cottage on Jahncke Avenue where a muscadine vine meandered over a huge pergola that shaded the entire back yard. Much of Kettye Malone's day was spent in a porch swing shelling peas or making fans of fragant vetiver as she sipped a cold Coke.

On The Avenue

Nana's house faced a thicket and yellow clay lane edged with deep drainage gutters evergreen with weeds. It was called 15th Avenue.

We used the rear entrance, a winding path in a narrow swath through wild greenery that now and then brushed the sides of the tan Studebaker. Enough sun peeped through to encourage honeysuckle and tangled patches of morning glory and wild berries.

My cousins and I were offered summertime rituals: there were snowballs at a certain time, dips in the cold river water in the mornings and late afternoons, daily showers in the big bathtub with iron claw feet, nectar sodas at Hebert's drugstore after Sunday Mass, and movies at night in Downtown Covington followed by helpings of grape jelly on Ritz, the new cracker sensation, on the rear screened porch.

There would be parties at the American Legion home on Jahncke Avenue, where teenagers learned to dance on Saturdays. There were fun hayrides in nearby fields under starry black skies.

The night's darkness was total and vast, the only light

came from stars that managed to shimmer through clusters of trees around the house. Half asleep a kid was lullabied by sounds of crickets, sometimes by the neighbor's chickens dropping from their roosts, or squirrels racing in the attic with their acorn caches. Once a curious cow came up to an open window to bellow.

Belching Pump

Always there were the humming sounds of the whirling ceiling fans, and the booming belches of the well pump under the house.

The house was of stained green cypress on the outside, and of tongue and grove cedar walls inside. Its roof was of corrugated tin. The lower window sashes were held open by small poles. The doors were seldom locked.

For the convenience of adventurous winter visitors there was a pot belly wood stove in the center room where we dined, listened to the radio and played Battle, or relaxed on couches and in rocking chairs. Food was prepared in a very basic kitchen equipped with a stove that used liquid fuel and a quaint kitchen safe that was filled with "depression glass" dinnerware. Every room had a kerosene lamp for when storms knocked out the electricity.

On 15th Avenue one might have encountered a goat who had wandered from home. Today the house on the avenue appears as a pastel colored storybook cottage that is air conditioned. The "country" has became a suburb where doors are locked.

'DADDY, THE ICE IS ON THE STEPS'

Children of the 20s and early 30s witnessed the birth of many wonders, not the least of which was the refrigerator. The ice box with its hidden pan that collected melting ice drizzle surrendered to the wizardly ice-maker.

At one time the likes of Sinclair Lewis, the President of the United States, Mary Pickford and some families in New Orleans had Frigidaires, a strange ice box that hummed and had no block of ice in it. It was something like physics, visible but not understood by ordinary folk.

Before the magical cooler came to our house the ice man came to a side kitchen door. "Ice maaaannnn," he'd call out. My mother would open the door, give him a coin and he'd shove the drippy ice block into the box. If no one was home when he called he dumped the ice by the kitchen steps.

If my mother was out playing auction bridge when the ice man came, the ice sat on the steps, melting. When she'd return she'd cover it with newspaper until my father came home.

"Daddy," she'd call when he stepped into the house, "the ice is on the steps."

He'd release the tie hold on his neck, take off his coat, pull on one insulated glove, get out his trusty ice tongs from under the sink and lift the big chunk of dripping ice from the steps.

"Try not to drip too much on the floor," my mother suggested as he jigged across the room, red faced and bent over. Sometimes the ice slipped from the tongs' grasp. Those were memorable moments.

When things went well the ice was slid into an insulated top compartment. Perishables were stored on shelves in a lower compartment. Underneath the box was the infamous drip pan that caught ice meltings. It had to be emptied periodically. The trick was to balance the large shallow pan of water while walking across the room to the sink. Sometimes that worked, sometimes it didn't.

The refrigerator, on the other hand, was pure luxury, and eventually the kitchen oddity that made humming sounds caught on and everybody had one.

When someone had a headache in a house with a refrigerator he simply placed its neat little ice cubes in an ice bag and applied it to the aching head.

In a house with an ice box it went this way: "Daddy," my mother would sigh, " please chop some ice for the ice bag. I have one of my headaches." There was an ice pick and scraper for such occasions and for making lemonade and mint juleps.

My dad's old ice tongs are hanging in my garage.

SUMMER AIR WAS STIRRED UP IN 'PURGATORY'

There are two or three generations among us who are unaware of what summer was like before air conditioning. It was like Hell. In another era New Orleans neighborhoods buzzed and hummed with the sounds of window fans, miracles of their day.

Before the great window fan was invented people were cooled by oscillating fans, if they stayed close enough to them. Five feet was too far away.

The circulating air fans did exactly what their name implied. They circulated air - all of it fresh from the heat of the sun.

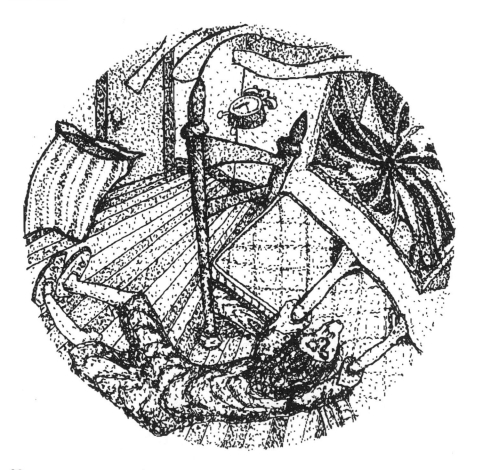

In my parents' room there was a tremendous circulating fan that blew air all over. It sometimes had pictures on the walls rattling, and lamp shades askew. That was some fan.

In my room was a small fan that buzzed furiously within a span of 10 inches. Shhhhrooom, shhhhroom, shhhhroom. Back and forth it went blowing hot air in the space it was designed to reach. Space outside the fan's reach was uncomfortably warm, not as hot as the proverbial Hell maybe, but close enough, more like what Purgatorial heat must be.

I mentioned the discriminatory fan distribution at our house, but it fell upon unsympathetic ears. "You're only one person," was the explanation.

Sammy the spitz did not count as a person. It was before the days of equal rights for animals and children.

Later, the grand window fan was introduced. It consisted of a framed set of large black blades that sat on a window sill. It ragged curtains and blew frail old ladies out of their beds. It also dragged in as much dust and grime as a storm. In essence it was a dust storm raging day and night for an entire season.

Certain windows and doors had to be opened or the furniture might have spun into a funnel to explode through the ceiling like unguided missiles.

A window fan was placed in just one room of the house. If there were fans in more than one room something sinister might have happened, I suppose. Perhaps the force of so much air would shake the house from its foundations and send whole families spinning to Oz .

In addition to tremendous currents of air, the window fan also rattled windows and dispensed an ear-shattering sound. The continual humming both lulled me to sleep and awakened me. For these reasons at our house the logical location for the fan was my room.

Every household had to have a window fan, or quiver from the menacing roar of his neighbor's window fan. These were the days before a neighbor could sue a neighbor for producing "menacing roars."

And then came the ultimate house cooler, the attic fan! The attic fan was placed in the ceiling of a hallway where its sucking sounds were muffled, somewhat.

Nevertheless, caution was advised. A person lying on a bed with a window open full and with the attic fan on "high" could suffer wind-burn, dry mouth and sniffles.

It was also a good idea to hold on to the walls when passing under the attic fan.

TAKING GHASTLY SPRING PURGE ... like a man

In the old neighborhood we knew exactly when we could discard our shoes and go barefoot on the hot pavement. It was the day after we took our so called "spring tonic." Unless it rained.

Also known as The Purge the tonic varied from household to household, but all were awful. It was one of those miseries dispensed for our own good.

"It's for your own good," my mother would assure me as she advanced slowly with a shovel of the cathartic.

The revolting procedure was necessary to "clean" us out, we were told. Some unfortunate kids had mothers who cleaned them out with two tablespoons of castor oil. I counted my blessings, tearfully. My dosage was a cooking spoon of magnesia laced with cascara, truly witch's brew.

I remember well how it was administered. I would be up against a wall, pleading, wailing, tears gushing, lungs expanding and contracting convulsively to expel thunderous screams as the giant spoon moved closer.

On one occasion, at age six or so, my mother had cornered me into an open kitchen window. I was crammed in crouch position on the sill, my back and head pushed against the screen. She came forward with the spoon. "You must take this. Take it!"

The phone rang but she continued approaching, balancing the nasty concoction.

"Th-th-the phone's ringing," I sobbed.

"Take this!"

It was in my mouth. I was going to gag on it.

"I have more if you spit it out."

It slid down

My eyes were closed, lips tightened as the icky potion slid down my gullet, gagging me.

My mother handed me the tainted spoon and picked up

the telephone, the 1929 kind that required two hands.

"Hell-oooooo," she said breathlessly as though taking time out from an exhausting waltz with Maurice Chevalier.

"Ohhhhhh, nothing. No. No. I was just giving him his spring tonic, Edna." It was the sweet lady from next door who never gave her children spring tonics.

"Yes, I know. He sits in the window when he takes it."

After the tonic it was time to go barefoot.

The whole neighborhood would be barefoot for weeks. Not exactly the entire neighborhood. Boys would be barefoot; girls wore their mother's old high heels.

When it was roller skate hockey season we'd rush inside to get our shoes and skates, go to City Park and gather some palmetto branches. From those we fashioned hockey sticks with saws, pen knives and sandpaper.

Artisans among us would meticulously carve a thing of beauty, as though it were intended to be forever. Some went so far as to wax the thing and carve their initials in it. All this made mine seem more mediocre, like those ill-fated balsam airplanes I labored over.

We sat on the street curb cutting and trimming and whittling. The first players finished went searching for pucks that were usually found in gardens and under houses. A perfect puck was a smooth rock shaped like a flattened egg.

Just about when we were finished carving our sticks and found a suitable puck we'd hear our names being called. Lunch time.

'Baloney & Chow'

We'd skate home, down a "baloney and chow" sandwich, an apple and a glass of milk and rush back to the roller skate hockey arena - the street in front of Charlie's house.

After a frustrating game of hockey that included yelling bouts and looking for the puck, we'd kick off our skates and shoes and run down to the Orleans canal.

We were warned many times, about 10,000 or so, not to go "down to the canal."

"Don't go down to the canal. There are snakes and broken glass there." Maybe it was 15,000 times we heard that.

In a bamboo thicket along the stream's bank we'd run up and down steep cement slopes, sometimes hopping over the water to the other side, always with one eye out for a snake.

We grew to manhood without ever having seen one. We never told our mothers that because they seemed to revel in their superior wisdom.

Tarzan Was There

Sometimes we searched for Tarzan and Jane, or head hunters. We tossed spears (hurriedly fashioned from the canal's bamboo woods) at "wild animals" that were always passing through the brush. We did this for hours until we heard a voice calling one of our names, or one of us cut his foot on broken glass, whichever came first.

At the sight of blood we could hear a mysterious authority deep inside us: "Don't go barefoot by the canal. There are snakes and broken glass there. You hear me? Don't go barefoot down by ..."

It was not easy to hobble home on one foot, holding the bloody one up, and then crying out, "Mama, I cut my foot." You knew the first words out of her mouth would be: "And where were you, Mister Smarty?"

Mister Smarty couldn't explain that. It was like Mister Smarty explaining having damp drawers and hair after a dip in the bayou.

AUNT MAMIE'S OLD HOUSE ON KERLEREC STREET HAD CISTERN & OTHER WONDERS

If you drive around in New Orleans' old neighborhoods long enough you may spot an ancient cistern. Sentimentalists keep them freshly painted and sturdy, as a bit of the landscape.

The cistern was once the Orleanians' principal water supply. In retrospect, it was a gross assault to common sense hygiene. Our forebears actually drank rain water that dripped from tin roofs into leader gutters to the big round wooden reservoirs with a tap at the bottom.

The only one I was ever close to in the city was on Kerlerec Street where my paternal great great Aunt Mary Cecilia "Mamie" Mayol Kernion, a widowed lady, resided with her old maid sister, Rosie. There also was Eddie Roach, always present and always called by both names, Eddie Roach. All three departed without ever having been asked who he was. My father never knew, his mother never told him, if, indeed, she knew. It was rude to ask. In later years I decided he was a boarder in Aunt Mamie's home, a situation that the lady felt was nobody's business.

Aunt Mamie had lots to say and could keep a one-voice conversation going without much effort. Aunt Rosie spoke hardly a word after "hello," and smiled and nodded her head until it was time to say "goodbye."

They lived in Victorian splendor with palms and aspidistra in great jardinieres, and large gilded mirrors over marble top tables. Aunt Mamie had married a man named Kernion, a shoot from the family of Jean Francois Huchet, Sieur de Kernion, who was among the few Frenchmen living in the small settlement near Bayou St. John 10 years before New Orleans was founded. At one time Jean Francois resided at the 1784 plantation house on the bayou, now 1300 Moss Street in the old neighborhood. Historians say the city's present day Kernions are descended from Jean Francois' grandson, Pierre. Aunt Mamie's husband, named for Pierre de Kernion, called himself Pete Kernion, even on his marriage certificate. The street where they lived, Kerlerec, was named for the Louisiana Governor Louis Billourd de Kerlerec (1753-62), a friend of Jean Francoise Huchet de Kernion.

I was a visitor at Aunt Mamie's home from babyhood until she died. My family regularly visited the old folks and brought me along. On many Sunday afternoons I became acquainted with great and great great aunts and uncles, second and third cousins. Visiting was what we did.

Behind Pickets

The cottage on Kerlerec Street was behind an iron picket fence hugged by roses in a plot along the *banquette*, and was like no other house I'd ever seen. An etched glass door at one side of the porch led the visitor along a long, narrow open railed gallery beyond which on one side was a garden with banana shrubs and sweet olive, and on the other a wall of shuttered French windows and doors that opened to the dining room and a bedroom. At the end of the gallery was a door to the kitchen.

From the street one could see the cistern plop in the middle of a bed of fern at the left rear of the house.

Even after graduating from high school I visited there with my parents, and recall the hugs and kisses of the two ladies who smelled of powder and cologne.

Visiting Aunt Mamie's was a rare treat for a small boy. She insisted that in addition to slugs of Jumbo drink I sip anisette or blackberry cordial she made.

We sat at a large round table in the dining room during our visits. From the tall mirrored sideboard Aunt Rosie took decanters, tiny glasses and dishes with cake and chocolates to the table.

"Aunt Mamie," my mother would say, "just a little for him.

He drinks it like punch. Just one. That's plenty."

The woman poured a little more into my glass. "He'll be fine," she'd say. She was right. I felt fine and always slept on the back seat of the car on the way home, sometimes clutching a silver dollar Aunt Mamie gave me.

Occasionally, Aunt Rosie would come from the kitchen with remains of a plump chicken, and we'd have sandwiches and root beer.

One day when I asked about "the big fat barrel" in the back yard, the two women laughed with their handkerchiefs to their faces. "Rosie, take him to see the cistern. He never saw a cistern? Mercy."

"He's seen the one at my aunt's farm in Houma," my mother told them.

Leaves & Rats

I followed Aunt Rosie to the fat barrel painted dark green with big metal straps around it. On top, she told me, was a lid and strainer to keep out "leaves and rats" and to make sure "that Mister Geranium (a big fluffy white cat who sat on pillows in a velvet covered chair during our visits) won't fall in."

I was anxious to leave before the rat arrived to excite the big fluffy white cat.

We'd have *cafe au lait* in small delicate cups and pastry before bidding the ladies farewell. They stood at a parlor window waving and blowing kisses.

"I'll bet they'll be snoring before we get home," my father said.

"Aunt Rosie had three of those blackberry drinks, and the sun is still shining," my mother added.

I would be stretched out on the back seat, heavy-eyed, but fending sleep to hear what was said. That's how I learned that a cistern was a filthy thing. My parents talked about it on the way home. "Here it is 1929, my dad said, "and they keep that old cistern when they have city water."

"Why we have none?" I asked.

"We have pipes under the house to deliver water," he said. "But when we were your age we had cisterns."

"No rats in yours, huh?"

"Rats! Well, I don't know. I never looked in it. God only knows what was in there."

The next week we'd go to see relatives in the Frantz family - my Dad's Uncle Buddy and his second wife Marie, from Paris, or Uncle Abby and his family. Sometimes we'd visit great Aunt Janie. There we'd see my father's cousins Eugene, Morris, Irene and Bob Mayol, my godfather. He sent me $10 with a card each Christmas until he passed away. Every two months or so we went to visit Aunt Eva Wright Salassi one of my mother's many maternal aunts. She was 90 years old and could walk, speak, hear and brew tea. "She was born before the Civil War," they told me. On Saturdays we saw Uncle Bill and Aunt Stella.

A few times each year we drove to Houma to see my mother's Aunt Nancy Wright Bergeron, her son, Bob, his wife Noticia and son Frankie at their farm and bakery on Main Street. A hospital is there today. There was a cistern near the side porch of the large old house. Tied to its spigot was a metal cup and ladle. Frankie and I drank water from it. It tasted "funny."

Beyond my age of recollection were visits to my relatives in Bogalousa in a Model T. Uncle Buddy and Aunt Dell, his first wife, lived on a farm. During one visit my Dad is pictured seated on the car's running board and I'm dressed in rompers and cap dropping corn kernels to ducks.

WHEN FREAKS LURED LITTLE BOYS

Rushing to the three-ring circus on the saw dust lot deep in the Irish Channel was an annual excitement.

Once a year when the heat wasn't at fry temperature and breezes weren't at hurricane watch velocity the circus came to town. It rose like a colorful hump out of place on a barren stretch of sand, dirt and crab grass along Annunciation Street near the old Mercy Hospital and a railroad terminal.

With the Mississippi River behind it the site seemed immense. The Big Tent was approached from a broad grassy walkway that was lined on one side by sideshow attractions. From colorful elevated platforms hawkers cried out the promise of derring-do by strange individuals behind the curtains. Patrons peered at the stages and the huge posters that invited them inside.

The circus kitchen tent, toasting peanuts, popping popcorn and the grazing animals gave off clashing odors that drifted to and fro with river breezes.

Each year - Nana, Uncle Jimmy, cousins Burdge and Mary Ellen and I, attended the event.

In Sunday Best

We'd arrive at the circus after Sunday Mass at St. Patrick Church, dressed in Sunday best, as was everyone else. Nana wore hat and gloves and Uncle Jimmy was in a seersucker suit, starched collar, tie and straw katy.

Inside the Big Tent we sat on the high-rise benches opposite center ring with cotton candy in one hand and a fistful of jelly beans in the other. We didn't do much applauding because there was always something in our hands - a Coke, peanuts, Popsicle or hot dog.

The Big Top was inches deep in sawdust, straw and animal deposits, the scents of which rose from beneath us where scavengers scanned for whatever might have fallen between the rickety floor cracks.

Aerialists performed daring feats at the tip top of the tent, elephants danced to Skater's Waltz and lions threatened to swallow their trainers. The music blasted as clowns twirled and flip flopped. They fired dogs from cannons and seemingly hundreds of men with painted faces and bulbous red noses tumbled from a tiny car that exploded on cue. We were mesmerized.

"After this are we going to see the bearded lady?" we'd ask.

I don't think Mary Ellen ever saw a sideshow at the circus. Either she was too young or the attractions too intense for little girls. Perhaps she didn't want to see them. But Burdge and I saw a selected few. Nana accompanied us. We were too young to go alone, she said.

Uncle Jimmy and Mary Ellen roamed aimlessly about watching animals in roped off areas. In the sideshows we saw some weird things - people with four arms that appeared to be glued together at the shoulders and cows with two heads, and men who swallowed flaming swords and ladies in gold dresses with sparkles who could tell people in the audience their ages. One sparkled lady pointed at Nana and said: "You, madam, have two children, one of those boys with you and a little girl outside the tent."

As we breathlessly related the tale to Uncle Jimmy he assured us "the whole thing is rigged."

"But Jimmy," said Nana, "the woman told me."

There was more candy, another Popsicle and soon we were in the car riding past large, elegant houses that lined the bumpy streets, and others where clothes hung on lines on the galleries, and with cardboard patches in windows where stained glass panes had been.

We drove farther and farther away until we no longer saw the Ferris wheel near the circus. We thought The Greatest Show on Earth really was.

THE GREAT DEPRESSION! THE GREAT WORLD WAR! A GREAT TIME TO LIVE!

A generation of Orleanians still with us spent their youth in the Great Depression.

They were toddlers at the advent of radio and talking motion pictures. As youngsters they played the first electric phonographs. As teenagers they marveled at streamlined locomotives and howled at the new Bugs Bunny. As young adults they were players in a World War. When they were parents television showed them men walking on the moon! At middle age they stepped gingerly into the Computer Age. As elderly folk they get courtesy discounts, but can't play their old Decca records. They saw the most outlandish technological advances in those most outlandish Flash Gordon serials they watched at the neighborhood show all become real.

Despite its name the Great Depression wasn't particularly depressing for kids. It was simply their time. The misery reported in newspapers and on radio seemed far away.

In our neighborhood Bosio's drugstore had a slot machine, soda fountain, and sold one Lucky Strike cigarette from a package for a penny. Mr. Olivier picked up our soiled clothing and delivered it fresh and clean hanging on a rod across the back seat of his Model-A Ford. The Imperial show charged a dime. The streetcar took you anywhere in town for seven cents. It was swell.

Pitiful Knickers

My most depressing memory of the Great Depression was having to appear in public attired in those pitiful looking knickers, argyle stockings and those Keds that grabbed the ankles. At a certain age it was goodbye short pants, but not quite time for hello long ones. There was that long-suffering in-between interval of the knickers. Those bloomers of wool in stripe and plaid designs were buckled just below the knee to secure the long argyles for a few minutes. Soon enough the buckle popped open and released the bloomers that flopped into a pile of wool below two nubby knees. The argyles slipped into furrows around two skinny legs piling at the ankle and on the tops of the boot-like Keds. Only adolescent boys were comic fashion figures. Boys didn't select apparel, their Mamas did. "Here are your new knickers and socks. Are your Keds holding out?"

Those Keds were worn for sport and support. Made of canvas they were laced from toe to above ankle where they were labeled with a KEDS patch. They were guaranteed to make a boy's feet sweat and his socks ... well, he tossed them outside on the back steps when he took off his shoes. The family dog and passing birds didn't go near them.

I associated the neighborhood barbershop with "hard times" for it was there that hard-timers assembled. The barbershop was an institution of depression, something like TV talk shows today. Mouths ran at a faster clip than the barber's scissors. Customers, mostly retired codgers with more nostril hairs than on their heads, spent Saturdays spewing words of wisdom and arguing any opinion that conflicted with theirs. Popular topics were Franklin Roosevelt, his wife Eleanor, Huey P. Long and the price of tobacco the stench of which permeated the shop.

Bottled Tiger

Lined up on a stained white marble shelf below a large spotted mirror that distorted reflections were a dozen bottles of mellowing Lucky Tiger cologne, a dish of razor blades, an ash tray and a small chest of barber tools. A huge jar of pomade promised to hold the most stubborn hair in place forever. There was enough hair on the floor to stuff mattresses for a dormitory.

"Yeah, ah know, lemme tell ya wuts the trouble wit dat

Roo -sa-velt. You wanna know wut's the trouble wit dat dere Roo-sa-velt? Ah'll tell ya ..."

As they yacked a staticky radio blasted: "And now the Babe is up and he's pointing to center field annnnnd ... he swings ... POP! ... and there it goes, roop, roop, roop - right on target - man alive, another homer."

"And dats wuts the trouble wit dat dere damn Roo-sa-velt. Doan evah tell me nuttin about him. Shhhhh ....."

Smokin' & Spittin'

All the men smoked, chewed on putrefied cigars and spat in brass cuspidors strategically placed on the floor. Frequently, they scratched mountainous bellies under tight shirts. Sometimes they removed their shoes to scratch their feet. "Man," they'd whine to the barber, "you sell somppin for boint up toes?" They thumbed through the Police Gazette, a magazine boys knew was not published for their eyes. But we could peek.

After an hour or more a kid left the shop, head hanging low with a gruesome cut, the kind that encouraged cowlicks to stand up proudly. A visit to the neighborhood barbershop ruined a kid's Saturday.

On the other hand, there were Ginger Rogers and Fred Astaire. They showed us how to make the best of a situation. They danced their cares away, he in white tie and tails and she in long gowns, both traipsing up and down staircases, leaping over sofas, sliding down banisters and in the rain. And Ginger did it all in high heels and smiling.

During the Depression children were more often seen than heard, except for obnoxious ones. It was a time when a boy rarely used the front door to enter or exit his home. Only the most brazen of them rang the doorbell of a friend's house. We called our friends directly from outside near an open window. "Ohhh, Tick-eee. Can you come out?" "Yeah, in a minute." Outside he'd say, "You woke up my grandma."

Soundaround

It also was the time when people heard outside noises from inside and inside sounds from outside, at least in summertime. All windows and doors were open and all radios were on. If a kid walked slowly for three blocks he could laugh at parts of Amos & Andy as he passed his neighbors' houses.

However tragic, the Great Depression had more pluses than minuses. Families were glued together. An array of loving uncles, aunts, cousins and grandparents sat around dinner tables and rocked on porches together. They bowed their heads when passing a church. A quart of milk in a glass bottle with a thick neck of cream at the top was delivered to the door.

Bread was nine cents a loaf, but you had to slice it yourself. Toasters were four-sided metal racks that were placed over a stove burner. Slices were placed on the rack to burn more often than not, then scraped of their blackness. Voila! toast.

Illustrations in newspaper ads were drawings, never photographs. When Herbert Hoover was president some cars had glass windows and some had isinglass ones that you rolled right down in case of a change in the weather. Before they moved, all automobiles had to be cranked by the driver or sturdy adult male passenger. The crank was inserted into the front of the car and the cranker gave it a whirl, another whirl and then another whirl and a harder whirl. Then he rested to catch his breath and continued whirling until the car started or he keeled over.

12 Cents a Gallon

Gasoline sold for 12 cents a gallon, and you didn't pump it yourself. The man who owned the "filling station" or his son pumped the gas, looked under the hood and kicked all the tires for you.

Things were so tough when Franklin Roosevelt became president that he introduced initialed government aided work programs such as NRA, NLB, CCC, WPA. One paid as much as $30 monthly and free room and board for labor.

I had free room and board, a dog, three pairs of argyle socks, and drank Ovaltine with cracked ice from an Orphan Annie shaker every day. And never did a lick of work, except bathe. It was swell.

A kid could guess which neighbors were rich. If they made at least $4000 a year they owned their house, didn't cut their grass themselves and disappeared to Carlsbad Cavern or Yosemite for three weeks as soon as summertime arrived.

Donald Duck was introduced to movies, and Dick Tracy and Blondie to "funny papers" when Depression kids were in grammar school.

President Roosevelt said on the radio that the South was the nation's top economic problem. The annual wage in the South, he told us, was about $865 when it was $1,291 nationally. The South was depressing the whole country, he said. We never knew that.

Reading 'Funnies'

On Sundays fathers read the "funnies" to their kids while their mothers changed from church clothes to prepare stewed chicken, mashed potatoes, green peas and lemon ice box pie for the mid-day meal.

There were pictures in the newspaper and in movie newsreels of long lines of people at soup kitchens and in breadlines. My most unforgettable Depression memories were those of "university students" in Latin countries pictured in the newsreels. The "university students" were forever shouting and marching with signs. We weren't sure what the problem was but hundreds of them banged heads with clubs and threw stones at police.

The movies had introduced a vamp, a tramp, a vampire and a platinum-haired bombshell. Just before the Great Depression Garbo had spoken on the screen for the first time. She said, "Gif me a viskey." We laughed at her in the neighborhood show. We didn't like Garbo.

With open mouths we watched Flash Gordon zoom in space, shooting ray guns at aliens and tracking foreign creatures on some kind of picture machine in his laboratory. We watched in awe the cockamamy plots.

All Kings

Fancying himself a contender for the U. S. presidency Huey P. Long topped Franklin Roosevelt's social agenda. Every man would be a king, he revealed in book and song. His Share Our Wealth program would tax wealth so that no family could accumulate more than $5 million. The garnished excess would buy every American family a house, car, radio and a few thousand dollars annual income.

In 1933 Roosevelt escaped an assasin's bullet in Chicago when that city's mayor was killed. Two years later the Kingfish (Long's moniker) was mortally wounded.

In New Orleans men walked the streets in our neighborhood ringing doorbells and asking for work. For a plate of red beans and rice from compassionate housewives whose husbands had jobs, the men raked leaves, trimmed trees, mended fences. I recall that my mother made "potted ham" sandwiches and iced tea for a man who came on a regular basis to perform odd jobs.

The 30s was an era when many boys were called "Junior" rather than by their given name which was the same as that of their fathers. Many others, for reasons unknown, were called by initials rather than their given names. As F.L. I didn't find that strange. I knew boys named G.C., C.G., C.J., C.A., J.L., S.L., A.J., G.W., T.J., H.L., R.J., C.R., R.N., L.J., J.D., B.J., two E.J.s, two J.C.s, and some I've forgotten. I know a woman named B.J. and another named D.A.

In 1934 John Dillinger became the FBI's first Public Enemy No. 1, after just a year of terror. It seemed longer. American Airlines announced that it would fly a plane that could travel 160 miles an hour and seat 21 passengers!

A curly-haired little girl with accentuated dimples became an entertainment phenomenon. Shirley Temple was 8 in 1936, already four years into tapping, smiling and pouting on cue. Every family wanted one.

I grew weary of hearing that tuition at high school was $10 monthly and that I wasn't applying myself. Jesse Owens broke all Olympic records in the dash and broad jump. Douglas Corrigan was to fly from New York to California but landed instead in Ireland. He was never called by his given name again. He became "Wrongway Corrigan." Yankee swatter Babe Ruth was inducted in the brand new baseball's Hall of Fame. He had a career of 714 home runs, 60 of which he claimed in one season.

Brown Bomber

Socko! The 23-year-old contender for the world's heavyweight boxing championship fell to the canvas in the first round. But he sprung to his feet. A minute into the eighth he pummeled opponent Jim Braddock so that his blood stained the floor. Joe Louis became the first black man in more than two decades to win the heavyweight title. He was called the Brown Bomber. That was in 1937.

Popular ventriloquist dummy Charlie McCarthy carried on so outrageously with oomphy Mae West in one-line radio vulgarities that NBC made a public apology. West and McCarthy went on to even greater fame.

In movie newsreels we saw a funny little man with a mustache and wearing a uniform and boots. He yelled and stomped his feet and always had one arm pumped high in the air. As far as one could see there were people, millions and millions of them, cheering. We laughed.

"Gone With the Wind" opened at the Loew's State where the box office line was the longest on record at 9 a.m. Girls in our neighborhood had read the book but refused to tell us about the naughty parts.

My favorite singer was Jo Stafford, of whom my father observed: "That woman doesn't sing, she moans. She gets paid for being miserable. Put that thing lower."

The Little Man

In the movies' newsreels FDR said that he and his wife Eleanor hoped that the U.S. could stay out of the war in Europe. We saw pictures of Britons fleeing for their lives to underground shelters to escape Nazi bombings. At the Imperial show I saw pictures of the little man with the Charlie Chaplain mustache on a balcony in Berlin yelling and stomping his foot and holding one arm high in the air. Millions cheered. I seemed to grow up watching that little man on the theater screens.

One Saturday night we learned where Pearl Harbor was while attending Loyola's German Club social at Perlin Meyers' house. The Japanese had delivered a sneak wipeout of the U.S. fleet there. The President of the U.S. came on the radio and told us we were at war with Japan and Germany (where that little man with the mustache was all those years). The Red Cross was baking doughnuts night and day. People bought War Bonds. Rosie became a riveter at shipyards. Men were called into service. Our neighborhood was stripped bare of young men.

On a Tuesday morning in July, 1943 I lived my regular life in the old neighborhood. The next day, on a Wednesday afternoon, life changed. A bus delivered us to a dusty plot on the Mississippi Gulf Coast called an induction center. It was in the middle of summer and the induction center was like an inferno. Following a brief but miserable stay in steaming hot tents there we traveled by train to the north-west coast. I was one of many who slept in the train car aisle. "We was overbooked," the man in charge yelled. Next stop: Oregon - a 14 day ride including breaks for Red Cross doughnuts.

I lived in a barracks, one of hundreds of dismal looking structures that were built in rows that extended for as far as the eye could see. On weekends we sat on cots waiting for passes to Corvallis. All of our feet were clad in the same style shoes, our bodies clothed in the exact same khacki cloth, and on our heads were identical rumpled caps. We did everything together – e-v-e-r-y-t-h-i-n-g – at the same time and side by side. We played pinochle, poker and solataire on our foot lockers at night, and exercised and hiked all day. Some days we walked deeper into the valley - six miles out for special "schooling". A likable sergeant from Brooklyn taught us "atomy and phyzology." We were infantry medics. Except when we slept there was never a moment of silence, never a moment of solitude.

I felt the sting of snow on my face for the first time one day when we assembled outside the barrackes for roll call. It was 6 a.m., dark and 10 degrees. We stood there, shivering, answering when our names were called. In the PX that night I got the Brown Bomber's autograph.

Dark Marseilles

A year later I was in France. At midnight we walked through the blacked out streets of Marseilles and into a clearance in the woods. There we pitched pup tents and shivered on the ground of ice. A light snow fell. The silence ended suddenly as three planes circled overhead, then dove, strafing the ice and snow-heavy trees. The planes were a few of the remains of the once mighty Nazi luftwaffe. We were assured the mission was planned as a nuisance, an attempt to scare us. Mission accomplished.

The next morning we boarded cattle cars and saw rural France in bright sunshine. Along the way I saw ruin and mostly aged people bent from the ravages of war and hard times. They waved to us with weathered hands. "American, American," they yelled. I saw absolute poverty over the land and in the peoples' eyes that seemed fixed with tears. Weeks later in Germany I would see big cities whose buildings and cathedrals were skeletons. The streets would be empty.

'Guten Tag'

On the occasion of our first Christmas in Europe we were quartered in what apparently was an abandoned and bombed radio factory in a hamlet in Alsace- Lorraine country. On Christmas Eve a buddy and I attended Mass in a small church a short distance from the factory and were on our way back when we came upon an elderly couple. They seemed to be holding each other up as they walked, he, a huge bearded man in tattered clothing, and she, frail and pressing a thin shawl across her face to ward off the icy wind. We exchanged greetings: "Guten tag," they said. "Guten tag," we responded.

At that moment we heard a buzzing plane. It circled above, then swooped toward us. Again and again it circled and swooped. Rat-tat-tat-tat. Ping, ping the bullets sounded against the church wall and street stones. The four of us ran hunched over and holding hands. We flung open the church door and threw ourselves on the vestibule floor.

The plane was higher and far away. We gave thanks in two languages. The couple pointed out their house a block away, and invited us to join them for dinner on Christmas. They told me they would kill their fat goose for dinner. The next day we dined in their kitchen, one step up from the stable that sheltered a cow, two hens and a goat. After dinner, a bottle of warm wine and a toast with schnapps they told us they hadn't seen their son in three years and had no word of him. When we were leaving the woman hugged us and sobbed. The man put his arms on our shoulders. There were tears in his eyes. They watched us from a small frosted window and waved to us. Don Conway and I waved to them. We wrapped our mufflers around our faces and kept our heads down to dodge the icy wind as we trudged in deep snow. Neither of us spoke.

Within a few weeks we were moving eastward in trucks and Jeeps toward the Rhine River. We learned that a dozen of our friends we trained with in Oregon had been killed or wounded. Replacements from England were joining us, the sergeant told us. Soon afterwards I would see men die, one with his head cradled in my arms.

During the cold nights when we slept with our clothes and boots on, I wondered how long the absurdity would go on, how many of us would not survive this craziness.

We sat on a slope along the Rhine River having coffee and read in the Stars & Stripes that FDR had died in Georgia. He was the one who was supposed to get us home again. Uniformed men cried when they read the news. But good news soon followed. The allies were in Berlin and the Nazis were running. The pitiful little man with the mustache was gone for good. No one saw him again.

But there was another war to win. All we ever heard was that Japan would never surrender. The rumor was that we would be leaving Europe for Japan.

It was up to President Harry Truman. He decided to drop two atom bombs in Japan. They demolished tiny bits of the enemy's tiny country and stunned the world. On September 2, 1945 aboard a U.S. battleship, Japanese emissaries dressed in tails and top hats and looking glum, formally surrendered.

The Great War had ended.

Things Changed

We returned to our neighborhood. My grandfather and

Sammy the spitz had died. Mr. Olivier didn't pick up our clothes any longer. The Imperial show burned down. Slot machines had been smashed with axes. Ordinary people had swimming pools in their backyards. Streets were filled with cars. Tall buildings rose like ducks in flight. We marveled at television. We took family movies with our Keystone camera and changed film under a bed or in a closet.

The Great Depression had ended.

For me The Great War and The Great Depression are not woeful memories. They were profoundly significant happenings in the human drama. I matured in those times. I learned a lot about people and faraway places, about good and evil that's everywhere. Some people everywhere nurture the former, some don't. I had gone into the war thing as a big boy and came out a young man with some gleanings of wisdom.

I also had tested trust and hope. I have vivid memory of being in a German forest when we broke ranks to rest. Soldiers were taught that whenever they slept in the open they should scoop out enough ground for protection and that they should sleep with helmets on. They should space themselves apart from others, they told us.

One night when our company trodded in a darkness lit by sparks from explosions in the sky, we made our way off the path to the foot of a mountain. "Aw-right, we'll rest here - no smokin," a voice shouted. "And spread out." With my pack shovel I scooped out part of the mountain base large enough for my helmeted head. I stuck my head in the hole.

A man named Nick was shaking me awake. "Tucker, Tucker (my Army nickname). Wake up. God-a-mighty man, how can you sleep with the shellin'? Come on. We're pulling outta here." He called to the others, all prepared to move out. "Here he is. He was sleepin'."

I was the comic relief for that day, and laughed with them. With my head in the hole, I told them, I could hear nothing.

116

The truth was that although I felt fearful helplessness with my head in that hole I murmured to a protector mighter than those exploding shells. In moments I found peaceful slumber in the foreboding darkness. Besides, I had always slept soundly, even as a tot, I'd been told.

On the voyage home, flat on my back with a Class A case of sea sickness, I read *Crescent Carnival*. I thought of New Orleans and all the dear people there waiting for me. I thought how lucky I was, how blessed.

On the ship I heard the voice of Jo Stafford singing on the radio, and thought: "That woman really is moaning." I could hardly wait to tell my Dad.

ENTER THE L-SHAPE, BYE-BYE TO PORCHES AND PIERS, SO LONG GARAGE, HELLO CARPORT

After World War ll there was peace and prosperity but there was a price. There'd be no new front porches in New Orleans.

The war veterans were home getting married, having children and were armed with the GI Bill that offered an opportunity to buy houses without down payments. Since the city's swampy outlands offered little space for immediate housing the initial large subdivisions were in neighboring Jefferson Parish.

There, when a man stepped aside a home builder erected a house on the spot where he had been. And a family bought it.

Hackberries in suburban Jefferson were bulldozed with record speed to make way for new houses on the swath. In a matter of weeks one home builder could add as many as three new street names to the map. Neither nook nor cranny were left without a house.

Three Tiny Ones

For the most part GI houses were simple rectangles with two small bedrooms or three tiny ones. To build affordable housing something had to go. First to go was the beloved front porch, the Orleanians' summer room.

From the front porch neighbor greeted neighbor, "How do."

"How do. And how is your mother-in-law today?"

"Uhh, *comme ci, comme ca.*"

The front porch was a grand New Orleans tradition. Families who resided on Louisa, Apricot, Elysian Fields, Galvez, State, Arts, Grand Route St. John or Prytania streets sat on their porches to catch a breeze, chat with a neighbor or fantasize in a rocker. It was an extension of the house,

118

and finicky residents had theirs screened. Others kept a can of Flit nearby to bombard flying intruders. Alas, the traditional porch has been downgraded to a monolithic concrete slab. Oh, the shame of it.

The porch went, but so did the garage. "And here is the carport," the real estate agent might say. "You can sit under here in the backyard with the car, and barbecue just as they do in California."

Nearly every prospective home buyer had an honorable discharge in his hand and enough money for closing costs in his wallet, but there was no porch, no garage.

After overbuilding on the West Coast, California builders came to New Orleans to introduce the joy of "informal living." Here was an opportunity to offer Orleanians something they had been missing for generations.They had porches, but they didn't have slabs. New Orleans families dwelt in houses on piers, high over the ground to fend off flood waters that came and went willy nilly. These traditional foundations kept their forebears' noses above water.

In quick order piers were out and slabs were in. And so was the water.

Rock in Carport

A generation or two of Orleanians and suburbanites have missed the allurement of the front porch where rockers, swings and ceiling fans in a gracious outdoor space kept occupants in touch with nature, but not too close.

Somewhere along the way Orleanians also lost an entire room of the house, the dining room, our forebears' gathering spot. To take its place builders introduced the L-shape, an architectural gimmick that somehow seemed appropriate for families speeding on elevated roadways and dining on quick foods from kitchen-to-auto-pass-through establishments. These are conveniently located in every block of the city and suburbs. Sometimes there are two in a block. Maybe three.

The agent showing the "demo" (a house just like one in the next block) almost always was asked, "Where is the dining room?"

The instant response was, "Oh. Here. We're in it. See? The L-shape. This is the L-shaped living-dining room with a pass-through to the kitchen. See? You can see the oven from the table. Aw-right, huh?"

The only reasonable explanation for the L-shape is economic. It eliminated a wall and arch. In the L-shape diners need not leave the living room to enter the dining room. They merely stand and walk into the bend of the L-shape where the table and chairs are.

At the height of its boredom the L-shape living-dining room was abandoned for "the den."

Pressed Together

It followed that after a few years of pressed togetherness in "the den" divorce rates were beginning to soar and minor children had their own keys to the house.

It was not uncommon to see an entire family in "the den" assembled around a TV set, seated on chairs and sofas, bean bags and the floor, each family member balancing a lap tray upon which was a heat-and-serve TV dinner.

There was much going on in "the den." Dad snoozed in the lounger with his feet up higher than his head that was red with blood. Mom sat in her chintz chair knitting and squirming in discomfort. Jefferson did his homework on the floor with a pen that leaked on the shag rug. Lulu Jean was on the phone getting homework assignment from the Soviet exchange student. The dog was watching TV.

Thus was "quality time" spent together during lap tray dining when everyone's favorite sitcom was on.

After gobbling down their food family members disposed of their aluminum trays and went to their respective tiny rooms to watch TV, snooze, knit, study and talk on the phone. Only the dog remained in "the den" on the lounger with its tail higher than its head.

CANTANKEROUS, PEACEFUL, LOVELY & SLOVENLY MAGNOLIA OFFERS TEST FOR PATIENCE

When Americans jigged the Charleston, sucked smoke from slender cigarette holders and suffered headaches and blurred vision in speakeasies, the popular writers of the day came to New Orleans to investigate that charming plot of charm - "da Quawda."

They came to eat the fabled food, reside in the quaint houses and bask in the balmy climate. It was an inspirational surrounding for the writer and artist.

They wrote about everything and painted everything, romanticizing every aspect of old and modern New Orleans. Everything was a subject for them - the cemeteries which they called "cities of the dead," the tester beds with mosquito nets, courtyards, lacy railed balconies, the Carnival, mafia, Creoles, saloons, cuisine, red light district, architecture, music, streetcars. And magnolia trees.

All mentioned the "magnificent magnolia", the "majestic magnolia", the "romantic magnolia", the "sweet-scented magnolia". There was no end to the litany of adjectives that described the magnolia tree. It was grand, stately and awesomely beautiful. They painted it, sketched it and took pictures of it. Tourists came just to see this remarkable tree.

The magnolia isn't all that remarkable. It was named in 1715 for French botanist Pierre Magnol. It appears in North America and Asia and is commonly associated with Old South plantations. Its blooms are large, showy and scented. And it drops leaves throughout its life span.

Not one writer points that out. No one has ever written that the magnolia's leaves drop off daily, day and night, forever.

It is comforting to remember that for all the years we celebrated together my wife and I did not argue seriously about anything. We simply disagreed over one thing or another at one time or another. Our disagreements were not about fundamental issues such as how to raise the children, or what tie I should wear, but of trivial things. The magnolia tree was one of those.

To me a magnolia tree was properly at home at the manor house of the plantation. There on limitless acres the trees stood tall and gracefully spreading, bearing their fantastically delicate, scented flowers. These fumes were breeze-propelled across broad verandas and into boudoirs and nostrils of wealthy inhabitants whose battalion of yard men raked the fallen leaves and blossoms the next morning.

It Was Perfect

Our first house, a tiny white cottage with a rose arbor on one side and another at the entrance, was perfect. All we needed, my wife said, was "a magnolia tree."

I ignored that.

But Happy wouldn't let it go. She said it again. I walked

out of the room. A short while later I heard her on the telephone. "I was thinking we could put a magnolia tree in the front yard. No. No. I did. No, he won't."

To this day I do not know to whom she was speaking, but I think it was a twit.

Time passed and we had developed a garden including banana trees and azaleas. It was perfect.

And then she said it. "If only we had a magnolia tree." I jumped in the car and went to the barbershop.

A few months later we were with friends and another couple we had just met. The female stranger told my wife, "And we have a little magnolia tree. I told Rastus that by the time it blooms we will have moved to another house, and he said that ..... blah-blah-blah." I never liked that woman, and upon learning that her husband had bought the magnolia tree, I didn't think much of him either.

That evening, when we pulled up in front of our house, my wife said, "Here. Right here. This is where we should plant the magnolia tree."

I said, "It's like that woman said tonight. We will have moved before the thing blooms. They are slow growers."

"They grow fast," she added.

The following spring we moved.

We were in a second house a few months when our son was born. When we came home from his christening, my wife said, "There. See, right there we can put a magnolia tree."

I Did Not Argue

I didn't believe she said that. But, of course, I heard her say it. She was going to say it again and again. I did not argue.

When the children were growing and the family required more space we bought our third house.

After settling in we planned a garden. On the afternoon

of the seventh day when we were relaxing and admiring our creation, my wife said, "We could plant a magnolia tree."

It was like a thunderbolt. And she added, "We won't be moving from here. We can grow old with our magnolia tree."

What could I say?

Howard Talen, the veteran nurseryman, was in our backyard suggesting where to plant trees. I knew he would tell us there would be no room for a magnolia tree after we selected the ash and the elm.

My wife clasped her hands together. "How about a magnolia?"

Mr. Talen frowned. "Hmmmm. You have that ash and that elm and those Japanese plums. Hmmmmm...."

"And they're so slow growing," I added.

"Oh, no," he retorted. "They grow fast."

"I told you they grow fast," Happy said.

"But, Mrs. Schneider," he said. "There is no space, you know, they get so big, so fast. And you ..."

"Ohhh, there's no place for one?" she asked, forlornly.

Right. That's what the man said. Too bad. That was it.

"Wait," the man spurted. "Let's see. Here. We could put a magnolia here."

What are you saying, you foolish person? Where? You just said there was no space and now there is? What happened? They grow fast and there's no room and now we can have one. Where?

He went on. "Here, near the edge of the house we can put a conical shape. It won't spread much. Yes. Yes. Here."

"Ohhhhh," my wife sighed, striking an angelic pose.

Not only did it grow tall but speedily, rushing toward the clouds at breathtaking pace.

In no time at all it was beyond the window of our second floor bedroom letting off sweetness into our nostrils, just like at the plantation manor houses so long ago.

I noticed that the tree dropped brown leaves profusely. All day and night they dropped (I actually heard them), sometimes to ankle-high depth in one day. I told my wife that the tree was sick and that we might lose it.

'That Tree is Sick'

"No," she said, "it's normal."

"You mean it is going to drop leaves forever?"

"In its season."

"It has four seasons. I rake leaves all year round. But they're falling more and more now."

"Well, it's a big tree."

"But it got big so fast."

"I told you it wasn't a slow grower."

I reported the sick tree to Mr. Talen.

"All year it has leaves. It never loses all of its leaves at the same time. They keep falling and coming back all year?"

"Sure. It's evergreen," he told me.

For 28 years I raked magnolia leaves morning, noon and at dusk, holidays, Sundays, Christmas Eves and on my birthdays. And I had to tangle with one of those threatening tree trimmers. Happy loved to "bring the blooms inside."

At the plantation manor house, or in magazines and in motion pictures the magnolia blossoms are huge, delicate and the palest cream color. But I can tell you that in real life when one of those creamy suckers get caught in a rake tooth you have a struggle on your hands.

One raking session can take from 20 to 40 minutes time, six trash bags, and two arthritic attacks. The real aggravation is bending over scooping up leaves when others are falling on your head.

For many years I considered the magnolia tree a curse. More recently I found it to be a means of acquiring the soothing virtue of patience. In time, it became a graceful bit of nature that invites me to rake its leaves in its deep, cool shade and ponder times spent with the sweetest person in my life, a New Orleans belle.

THE OLD TOWN IS PAROCHIAL, SEASONED, QUAINT, ROMANTIC, PEERLESS, SPIRITUAL, FAMOUS, HISTORIC, FUN & *JE NE SAIS QUOI*

Modern New Orleans, 278 years in the making, remains tightly knit and hemmed in by water which is both blessing and curse.

The casual observer might consider the native a strange bird who is a tad slow and with speech that belies Deep South ancestry. Heat and humidity may account for the slowness, and the dialect is a gumbo that comes from dumping many languages into a melting pot, much like what happens with ingredients in Creole soups.

It's likely that the natives are merely weary. They survive the formidable challenges of living in a bowl below sea level by floating in floods, racing from hurricanes and dodging thunder storms, all the while managing to secure parking spaces for countless street parties.

Accustomed to such stress the native develops a cautious outlook. A we-are-already-perfect-thank-you attitude pervades urban thought. Woe to the migrant entrepreneurial wizard who arrives with plans to build the biggest and best of something or other.

The townspeople cry out in unison, "Get thee to Houston!" Many a World Class Very Important Promoter has lain awake nights in his hotel room trying to understand the native mind. Perhaps the stubbornly traditional Creoles, our *ancienne population*, initiated our resistance to change.

Whatever one may think of the city's fossilized thought it is precisely because of it that the French Quarter remains intact and without an elevated interstate highway sprawled along its riverfront. Watchdogs are forever on alert for intruders.

Age alone earns New Orleans the title sage and so she makes these enchanting claims, boasts of these romantic truths, spins these engaging tales and *je ne sais quoi,* I don't know what:

THE *BANQUETTE* (bank-et) is what we walk on when outside. There are no banquettes in Memphis, Dallas, Baton Rouge or Paris. The French colonists jovially referred to the town's original city blocks as "islands" since often there was so much water around them. The wooden walkways around the islands' banks were called *banquettes* - "footpaths on the banks." It is not a sidewalk. The French word for sidewalk is *trottier,* a word never used in New Orleans.

RUE is the French word for street. So there were *rue Dauphine, rue de la Chartres* and so on. When Spain owned the town *rue* became *calle,* Spanish for street. Americanization did in *rue* and *calle* but recent city fathers have identified streets in the old Quarter as *rue* because such romantic stuff intrigues visitors.

THE WHATEVERS. The French called their flagstone-floored and walled backyards *cours,* courtyards. When the Spanish came the *cours* became *patios.* Natives use both terms without being certain whether or not there is a difference. Many natives have backyards with chain link fences in lieu of brick walls and crabgrass instead of flagstones.

THE GALLERY. By definition a gallery is an upper-level porch but Orleanians use the word to indicate porch wherever the location. The French colonists had a *galerie* on the second level of his house. The Spanish house had a *mirador,* balcony. So Orleanians have galleries and balconies, courtyards and patios. But few are aware of the differences.

IRON LACEWORK rails on galleries and balconies, often fancy and distinctive, are of two kinds. The more costly wrought iron ones resist rust. Those of cast iron are prone to rust. But to the average Orleanian all are "wrought iron". It is widely accepted that the handsome wrought iron rails in early construction were imported from Spain. Some prefer a more romantic source: the Lafitte brothers' (the pirates) slaves forged them locally. The average Orleanian couldn't care less.

LOUEEZY WHO? In grammar school we were taught that Louisiana was named for King Louis XIV and his mama, Anna of Austria. LaSalle named the territory *Louisiane* which means "land of Louis." When the Spaniards came they changed the name to the Spanish *Luisiana*. The United States renamed the state using portions of its French and Spanish names - "Louis" and "iana." Orleanians give no thought to such things.

B.C. (BEFORE CARNIVAL). Before the organized Carnival in New Orleans the Creoles waltzed in their parlors, and sipped wine with friends and family during the season preceding Lent. Papa played the violin and Celestine the piano. Perhaps the twins Lilia and Adenise would sing. It was a splendid opportunity for young ladies to meet young gentlemen in a controlled environment. All *meres* present were swollen with pride and weighted with anxiety. *Peres* eyed young suitors warily. Nearby, the hoi polloi found their amusement at a dance hall on *rue Conde* (Conti) between Dumaine and St. Ann streets. Admission was 50 cents for chaperones who watched the dancers from box seats. Usually the musicians were a handful of gypsies with violins. Boys met girls. Early public observances at Carnival time were little more than street shenanigans where onlookers were sacked with flour, and spirits flowed faster than rainwater in the gutters.

TUESDAY IS FAT. The Carnival season begins after Christmas and ends with Mardi Gras, the day before Ash Wednesday of the following year. Sometimes it seems longer. Mardi Gras is always a Tuesday. Mardi means "Tuesday" and Gras means "fat." There can be no Mardi Gras Day just as there can be no Tuesday Day but you will hear it said and read it. After experiencing one Mardi Gras the merrymaker knows why it's called Fat Tuesday. Rex is King of the Carnival. He is Rex, not King Rex, for the same reason there is no Mardi Gras Day.

"COCTAY" IS BORN. In Old New Orleans it was common for Creole gentlemen to meet at an apothecary's shop for conversation and wine. A popular one of its day was that of Antoine Amedee Peychaud who migrated from Santo Domingo. His shop was at 437 *rue Royal*. He found instant success not so much because of his medicinal remedies but for the bitters he concocted. To cognac, Peychaud added a dash of his bitters (named for him) for extra kick. He used an egg cup to measure the ingredients. The Creoles called the cup in which they served soft eggs *coquetier* (ko-k-tay). As happens in New Orleans it was mispronounced by many as "coctay." The drink the pharmacist served became known as a "coctay." In time the man's spiced brandies were called "cocktails." That's the way the story goes.

YOUR JULEP, SUH. Magnolias, moonlight, honey chile, manor houses and rural cabins all stir sentimental flashes of the romantic Old South. The Mint Julep is Old South with a boot. The Virginians claim to be the originators. So do Kentuckians, Georgians, Marylanders and Louisianians. It could have originated anywhere it's so simple. It's whiskey with a little simple syrup, mint and ice.

One places a silver goblet in the freezer and when it's frosted pours into it a bountiful amount of Bourbon, pounds some sugar, a trickle of water, and mint leaves that is added to the cup which is packed with ice, and jiggled. Sip ever so slowly. After the first you may choose to skip the mint and sugar. The most restrained guest will not know the difference. Some suggest you use rum, or rye whiskey, but you would not be drinking a genuine New Orleans Julep. New Orleans gentlemen (many when off to the duel) preferred Bourbon.

They were drinking Mint Juleps in Louisiana before 1800, and it is believed they were introduced in New Orleans originally using rum and sugar cane syrup in 1793 when French aristocrats came from the Caribbean. One Orleanian wrote in 1804: "The first thing he did upon getting out of bed was call for a julep and I date my own love for whiskey from mixing and tasting my young master's juleps."

THREE ... oops, FOUR DOMINIONS. Plaques on two long rows of street light standards on Canal Street note that New Orleans had three owners: "French Dominion,1718-1769; Spanish Dominion, 1769-1803; American Dominion, 1803-1861 to date." No mention is made of the Confederacy era. Actually, it was at two intervals under domination of the French. The Spanish did not own the town in 1803 when the Louisiana Territory was sold to the United States. It was ceded to Spain in 1769 but was subject to France again in 1801 until sold by Napoleon in 1803. So?

WORLD'S BIGGEST CITY. When the World's Industrial and Cotton Centennial Exposition was held in New Orleans in 1892 the city was the largest in the world in land area. It covered 155 square miles, six square miles more than London, seven times the area of New York City and 26 square miles more than Philadelphia. A lot of it was swamp but that fact isn't printed in the exposition's souvenir Visitor's Guide. The city then was lighted by 4,559 gas lamps, 2,000 oil lamps and 482 electric bulbs. When the city was founded in 1718 the population was 118. It was 250,000 when the exposition opened in Audubon Park. Visitors paid $4 a night to stay at the grand St. Charles Hotel (an exquisite, historic edifice demolished recently for progress). For just $2 visitors stayed at Strange's Hotel in the first block of Chartres. They came by train from Atlanta for $14.90 round trip and from Niagara Falls for $30.25.

Twenty years before the Exposition New Orleans was made up essentially of residential neighborhoods that hugged the river. These expanded beyond the Quarter's City Hospital and Esplanade Avenue to the Marigny section and Elysian fields Downtown. Uptown growth was beyond St. Charles to the Claiborne Canal in some areas, and had spread to the town of Carrollton at the river's bend. In Midtown people dwelt along and off both sides of Canal street for some distance. On the West Bank, beginning at what is Algiers Point today across the river from the Vieux Carre, was a community known as McDonoughville.

Aside from these growth areas most of the official map of the city in 1872 is noted as "oak forest", "swamp" or "cypress swamp". In one spot was a "brush swamp". At a point lakeward of the Claiborne Canal (now North Claiborne Avenue) were vast open areas belonging to families, widows and heirs of families, or to those who claimed ownership.

My old "back of town" Bayou St. John neighborhood then was labeled as parcels belonging to "widows and heirs" of Francois D'Hemecourt, F. Bethancourt, Gabriel Fondgergine, J.L. Alpuente, M. Courcelle, J. Vienne and others. Two blocks from where Sammy the spitz and I would dwell 60 years later was a plot along the bayou labeled "Magnolia Garden." There are magnolias there today. Nearby were Greenwood, Cypress Grove and St. Patrick cemeteries and Boys House of Refuge.

Back of "back of town" - that would become Lakeview - was described as "swamp", and most of it was owned by Alexander Milne, for whom a long Lakeview thoroughfare is named. Not until early 1900s would farmers and dairymen venture into Milne's swamp.

Interestingly, the 1872 map of the city bears an exact likeness to a map that was commissioned in early days of the Civil War. This earlier map is described as "meticulously accurate" and was prepared by order of Union Maj. Gen. N.P. Banks. The map is dated Feb. 14, 1863 when New Orleans was viewed by Yankees as a strategic military possession.

Besides "roads and railway lines, canals and fortifications", it shows the formidable swamps and forests "that were still to be conquered by the spreading city."

FRYDY EVE-NIN. For tens of thousands, maybe more, of native Orleanians the days of the week have no "day" sound in them. They are Sundy, Mondy, Toosdy, Wenzdy, Thoizdy,

Frydy and Saddy. As the days follow one another they turn "ta-maw-rahs" into "yes-titys." Battalions of Orleanians are unaware of afternoons. Any time after noon is "eve-nin." At some point "eve-nin" turns to night, but no one is certain at precisely what time that occurs.

FILE' (fee-lay) is a tasty thickening agent added to French Creole gumbo (a kind of soup) after cooking is complete. It is made from dried, powdered sassafras, a popular herb grown by Indians in Colonial Louisiana. It is still used in traditional French oyster and meat gumbo. It is added to the bowl of soup just before serving, never to the pot. Cooking makes it stringy.

AMUSING MUSES. The insufferably correct among residents of the city call the street named for the Greek muse of tragedy Melpomene as Mel-pom-e-nee, as does most of the world. Locals, including electronic reporters and those who reside on Melpomene Street call it Mel-po-meen. Another street, Terpsicore (muse of dance) properly pronounced Terp-sic-hory is Toip-si-core to many Orleanians. Euphrosine (one of the three graces) pronounced U-phros-iny becomes U-fro-zeen in New Orleans. And Caliope, muse of heroic poetry, is not Cal-eye-opee, as might be expected, but Cal-ee-ope. One can hardly get quainter.

JIMMY WHOEVER. When talented Irish architect James Gallier came here from Ireland his name was Gal-ee-er, as the Irish said it. In the 1800s he built some of the city's grandest landmarks, admired today, including a house built of many advancements for himself on Rue Royal. Quickly New Orleans made him French by calling him Gal-yea. Some speculate that Gallier (still called Gal-yea as in Gal-yea Hall) encouraged that pronunciation to win more contracts.

VOO WHO? Two words most absurdly pronounced in New Orleans are those that refer to the city's initial neighborhood along the river the Vieux Carre (Old Square). The French words are properly pronounced Vee-yur Cah-ray but many learned say Voo Caw-ray. Local politicians have had hot discussions about things going on in the Vieux Carre. "We just can't have another one of them Voodoo shops in the Voo Caw-ray." Some prefer to call the Vieux Carre "French Quarters" as though there were at least two original cities. No one is very concerned about this. From the beginning the name was confusing. Bienville engaged Adrien de Pauger to lay out the first streets in the town. In 1723 initially he drew his map roughly in the shape of a parallelogram. There we have it: the original city plan was an Old Parallelogram.

WUT-CHA-SED? An Orleanian might be overheard telling his friend in a cafeteria: "I gotta go wrench ma hanz inna zink." A linguist might tell us that such sounds occur in a melting pot. For the same reason, before entering first grade an Orleanian must complete "kinnygawdin." It follows that the first mausoleum built in New Orleans in the 1930s was called muz-OLE-eeum by many. Some hang their clothing in lockers, not closets, although, indeed, their clothing hangs in closets, not lockers. There is also the spread known as "my-nez" which has been hanging on for generations. It's used in egg salad or on a sandwich, a.k.a. "sam-mitch" in some circles. And there's Gawd, dawg and gawd dawg. Everyone knows that Punchatrain is a big lake. Unfortunately, the big lake is too often a "terlit" and isn't fit to swim in unless you "berl" the water. Earl is a man's name when capitalized. When lowercase "earl" is a substance used in cars or on salads. Fried "ershtas" is the Orleanians' *piece de resistance.* You get the pernt.

CREATIVE TALK. All cities have medians, safety zones between traffic lanes. New Orleans has none of these, except from the mouths of recent residents. New Orleans has "nootroo grouns" (neutral grounds). Example: "Hurry, we can run to the nootroo groun before that caw hits us." It makes sense. The label "nootroo groun" probably came because of a wide stretch of dirt that predates Canal Street, which was never a canal. At one time it was suggested that a canal be dug where Canal Street is. This piece of ground became a median that separated the old French city Downtown from the new American sector Uptown. It belonged to neither side, truly a neutral ground. It follows that Orleanians would call all medians, the centers of all its boulevards, "nootroo grouns'.

BARBARIAN'S VISIT. New Orleans escaped damage from the war. Which war? THE WAR. Though it escaped Atlanta's fate, the city took on and licked Gen. Benjamin Butler during Reconstruction, albeit occupation. Quickly labeled "Beast", the general, a rather unattractive and ill-tempered fellow, was inflicted upon the city as administrator and peace keeper.

At one point Union occupiers also took on the Jesuits when a New Orleans woman made a gift of her fine French candelabras to Immaculate Conception Church on Baronne Street. Perhaps she did so to protect them from the "beast" who was also called "spoons" because sometimes in lieu of taxes he confiscated silverware from New Orleans homes. However, she claimed otherwise.

One of Butler's officers appeared at the church one day demanding the pair of candelabras which he called "rebel property." Pastor Aloysius Curioz, S.J. insisted they were church property and refused to surrender them. As he protested the officer snatched the candelabras from the altar.

Accompanied by the French Consul, Father Curioz marched to Butler's office demanding that the treasures be returned. The priest was taken aback when Butler ordered the offending officer to return the candleabras to the church. Pastor Harry Tompson S.J. recently removed the candleabras from hiding.

What really irked the general were "the women of New Orleans." His diary reads: "On the evening of the third day after our occupation of the city, the colonel of the 31st Massachusetts Regiment called upon me and said: 'General, as I was walking down Canal Street, a young lad of say 10 years, in the presence of his mother, who is the wife of one of the first (important) lawyers, rushed from her side and spit all over my uniform.'"

Butler summoned Mr. P. the prominent lawyer, and told him of his son's behavior in the presence of his wife, whom Butler described as being "exceedingly interested on the side of the rebels". He suggested that the father dispense proper punishment to the boy.

He also wrote that his troops complained of ill treatment by women. One woman flung herself from the banquette and into the gutter when two Yankee officers approached from the opposite direction. When they offered to assist her she yelled, "Don't touch me! I'd rather lie in the gutter." Another officer got into a streetcar and three women jumped from the car with "every sign of disgust, abhorrence and aversion."

Another Butler account: On the sabbath when a Yankee officer walked to "divine service" with prayer book in hand, a woman passing by spit in his face. Such "audacious actions" by New Orleans women prompted the general to post in the streets his infamous May 15, 1862 order:

"General Order No.28: As the officers and soldiers of the United States have been subject to repeated insults from the women (calling themselves ladies) of New Orleans, in return for the most scrupulous non-interference and courtesy on our part, it is ordered that hereafter when any female shall, by word, gesture, or movement, insult or show contempt for any officer or soldier of the United States, she shall be regarded and held liable to be treated as a woman of the town plying her avocation."

Butler's chief of staff cautioned that the order might be misunderstood, and that "great scandal could result if only one man should act upon it in the wrong way."

To that Butler replied, "Let us then have one act of aggression on our side. Here we are, conquerors in a conquered city ... and we cannot walk the streets without being outraged and spit upon by green girls."

Order No. 28 was the source of much controversy and some historians wrote that Butler took pleasure from the anger aroused by his command. Public revulsion toward his action was widespread. The Premier of Great Britain wrote to an English statesman: "I will venture to say that no example can be found in the history of civilized nations, till the publication of this order, of a General guilty in cold blood of so infamous an act as deliberately to hand over the female inhabitants of a conquered city to the unbridled license of an unrestrained soldiery."

Shortly after the incident Butler was removed from his New Orleans post less than seven months after his appointment. He went on to become governor of Massachusetts and an unsuccessful candidate for the presidency of the United States.

Before leaving town, however, the frowning general approached the pastor of St. Patrick Church on Camp street and expressed his annoyance that Father James Mullon refused to bury Yankee soldiers from the church. "Sir," the pastor responded, "I have no objection to burying all of your men, and you too, sir, with great pleasure."

WHAT'S IN THE COFFEE? At one time, after being weaned, the New Orleans child was given *cafe au lait* - coffee with milk that always was boiled. Youngsters who clung to their bottles for an interminably long period sucked cafe au lait from them. Children often were treated to coffee in mid-mornings and mid-afternoons as families sat around kitchen tables. The childrens' cup was more milk than coffee to cut the sting of tar-black chicory. There are two brews in the New Orleans households: pure for sissies with abdominal sensitivity, and chicory for the stalwart. Serious drinkers take theirs black without sugar. Locals have been known to drink two pots a day - to settle their nerves.

Chicory is an additive, a flavorer. It gives New Orleans' traditional coffee a kick to flavor and color. Usually 10 percent of the mix is chicory, but old timers and bayou people like theirs a bit stronger, maybe 20 percent or more. Many New Orleanians are unaware of what chicory is and fewer care. It' a thick-rooted herb grown as a salad ingredient or dried, ground and roasted for use with coffee.

I LOVE *ROUX*. *Roux*, French meaning browned butter, is pronounced just as is the word for street - *rue* (roo). It's the thickener and flavorer in many Louisiana dishes. Basic ingredients are butter and flour that are browned in a pan or skillet to which is added chopped green pepper, onion, celery, garlic, all sauteed and used as titillating foundation even for the lowly canned green pea. A typical Orleanian can detect at once whether or not a dish has a *roux*, though he may not be able to spell the word.

A SQUIRT OR TWO. The Orleanian's obsession with food is in his genes. Earliest residents concocted spicy meals. Today countless kitchens are stocked with a cooking aid that is as essential as the black iron skillet or flour for the *roux*. Seldom does gumbo (a soup) or jambalaya, red beans, stuffed peppers, raw oysters, fried shrimp or a Bloody Mary enter the Orleanian's mouth without a squirt or two of TABASCO.

The pepper sauce industry began in 1868 when Edmund McIlhenny developed "the perfect pepper" on Avery Island where Gulf of Mexico waters splash on Louisiana's swampy shore. In 1888 the strain developed by McIlhenny was identified by botanists as "tabasco peppers," a subspecies from red peppers. The seedlings are transplanted from greenhouse and hotbed to the field. After harvesting they are crushed, blended and bottled on the island, the McIlhenny clan home since 1818.

MERCI DIEU. There were French settlements in the Louisiana Territory before New Orleans was founded in addition to the area near Bayou St. John, the Indians' hunting and fishing paradise. There were forts at Mobile Bay, Dauphin Island off Alabama's coast and at Biloxi. Bienville considered these locations too storm-prone or of shallow

138

harbor for a colony that would enter into fur trading. He wrote letters to the powers in Paris beseeching them to change the seat of government westward to the banks of the mighty river. Voila! New Orleans.

WHAT'S A CAJUN, FOR TRUE. A Cajun is the sound of the word Acadian (ah-cah-djen). The Acadians are Frenchmen whose ancestors settled in the Canadian Province of Acadia, now Nova Scotia, in the early 18th century. When the British arrived there the French were expelled, and many migrated to Louisiana as early as 1764. Their courageous adventure to Deep South country is immortalized in Longfellow's classic *Evangeline*. One Cajun friend, Clyde LeBlanc, in his singularly delightful book on his heritage - The Nobell Letters - writes: "I noted that the most evident and important Cajun characteristics are a sense of fraternity, a sense of responsibility and a sense of humor." Also Cajuns introduced spicy hot foods to the world.

LAGNIAPPE, pronounced lah-nyahp, means a little something extra that is free. Lagniappe was common in Creole times in New Orleans when butchers and street vendors wrapped a little more than a pound or a dozen. I recall the corner grocer giving me licorice sticks or suckers when I picked up my mother's order for a pound of this or that.

OLDEST IN WORLD. The St. Charles streetcar line is the oldest continuously operating urban transit of its kind in the world, and was first of its kind in America. It appeared on St.Charles Avenue on February 9, 1833. At one time the entire east bank of the river was serviced by the airy streetcars. For pennies a passenger could hop aboard a streetcar and ride and rock all the way from one limit of the city to another. In more recent years all the tracks were ripped up and the streetcars sold to cities all over the world. They were replaced by lumbering, fumey buses that compete with cars for street space. Exalted ones said it was progress. Streetcar buffs became infuriated and jumped up and down shouting in front of TV cameras. As a result we got to keep the one streetcar, the old St. Charles line. Today, society's two great Ps - Planners and Politicians - seriously consider the Herculean task of returning tracks so that new streetcars can replace buses. They say it's progress.

ORIGINAL CANDY. The praline was the Creole's favorite candy and they brought the recipe from France. It is named for Count Plessis-Prasline, a French soldier in 1675. Always patty-shaped the original pralines consisted of sugar and crushed almonds that were boiled until the sugar browned. Unfortunately, there were no almonds in Louisiana. The Creoles substituted whole or crushed pecans, abundant in Louisiana. The New Orleans' 1800s kitchens reeked of the scent of the thick, syrupy mixture boiling in kettles. Blacks continued making pralines through the years and sold them from large baskets on their arms on French Quarter *banquettes*. One commercial praline maker's logo was the likeness of a traditional mammy with tignon and apron. All of that has disappeared but not pralines. They come in all sizes today and include chocolate ones. Some are delicious, some so-so. Consistently good are those made by Tee Eva (along with pies) in her Magazine street kitchen. For lagniappe she speaks with a "Frenchy" accent.

THREE FRENCH TONGUES. The Creoles in New Orleans spoke pure French, sometime referred to as Parisian French. The Cajuns speak their own French dialect in Louisiana. Gombo French (as distinct from gumbo, the soup) is French spoken incorrectly, a patois.

DUELING UNDER THE OAKS. The Creole gentleman would duel at the drop of a hat, or less if he had a mind to. He was of inflexible will, and demonstrated keen talent with the sword. He enjoyed dueling as his wife enjoyed expressing her social skill at *soirees* in her double parlors.

As sinister as dueling sounds, participants didn't always bleed to death on the field. Many challengers often were satisfied with the sight of blood, a nick on the cheek - upper or lower - often sufficed.

140

Initially duels took place in the secluded garden behind the cathedral, just a short trip from home for challenger, offender and accompanying friends. Fencing schools, staffed by Paris' best, were numerous in the French Quarter.

As the city expanded duels were fought under particular oaks at City Park, a pleasant trip by horseback or carriage. The esteemed City Park Dueling Oaks are still growing, assisted by supports sufficient to counter their infirmities brought on by storms and age.

French and Spanish duelers preferred the pointed rapier or other swords and sometimes the curve blade saber. The Americans introduced the pistol.

PARRAIN & MARRAINE. The chance people known as *parrain* and *marraine* exist outside Louisiana in America is remote. They could only exist in certain cultures that are fortified with pride, devotion to the mother tongue and traditional way of life. Such were the societies of the Creoles and the Acadians in Louisiana. The *parrain* was the godfather and *marraine* the godmother for little Pierre or Elise. Custom dictated that the proud parrain give the child a suitable memento on the occasion of his Catholic birth and heritage, such as a sterling food bowl or cup. And he offered a donation to the priest who baptized little Pierre. *Marraine* gave Elise a crystal rosary or gold cross for her First Communion. In exchange the godchild owed his *parrain* and *marriane* a lifetime of devotion and respect. Pierre and Elise were reared that way, as had been *parrain* and *marraine* before them.

WHEN FRENCHTOWN SHUNNED. The old French Quarter the Creoles loved was not always such a grand place to live, though the most stubborn of the French remained there until after World War 1.

At one point in its history the French Quarter was commonly called Frenchtown. It had lost most of its attractiveness, and locals visited there only to attend Mass at the cathedral, dine at one of its few fine French restaurants, or attend performances at the French Opera House.

In the 30's young ladies were given specific instructions by their mothers never to enter "Frenchtown." To be there was risky. As late as the early 1940s mothers still were suspicious of Bourbon, Dauphine and Decatur streets. Mostly tourists shopped the Royal Street shops where bargains were abundant.

More than a decade earlier the Quarter was little more than a slum, and recovery was long coming. When at its worse cows grazed in the lobby of the deteriorating St. Louis Hotel, a casualty of a storm, and other animals roamed the Pontalbas.

There were tales of rape, murder, white slavery and gang fighting. The city's fabled restaurants operated in an atmosphere of cheap wine, gin and dope. Once beautiful residences of the Spanish upper class were tenements. Courtyards and patios were bare except for garbage, dogs and clotheslines. Chickens ran loose and manure was plentiful.

Prostitutes stood naked behind shutters purring to passersby. When the French Opera House burned all were certain the old historic district would die. It seemed it would never return to glory. La fin.

Between two world wars the Age of Bohemianism arrived, and the Quarter seemed a natural place for artists. Writers came from everywhere to tell of the Quarters charm and magic. Lyle Saxon, a noted New Orleans writer, moved into the Quarter, and his articles in *The Times-Picayune* urged people to reinvest there.

Local and foreign writers, artists and poets moved in. Potted geraniums, banana trees and trickling fountains returned to the courtyards, and rockers and potted plants to the galleries.

The Vieux Carre Commission, a state creature, was established as the official watchdog before which every owner, tenant, entrepreneur, lawyer, contractor and architect with any sensational ideas for improvements must appear.

A PECULIARITY. Louisiana is the only state in the U.S. without a single county. That's because it stubbornly held on to the Roman Catholic French and Spanish systems of using the ecclesiastical "parish" boundaries as civil ones. Oleanians are crazy for custom. No Louisiana Purchase could change that.

THAT HANGING STUFF. Those silvery, lacy drippings seen mostly on the ancient oak trees here is moss, also called Spanish Moss though it doesn't appear in Spain. It appears in Deep South states and also in the West Indies. For a long time it was considered parasitic, but it isn't. It is a plant of the pineapple family that is air grown. It may be removed from a tree and placed on another and continue to grow. Early rural families collected it with poles, air dried it in sunshine and made mattresses of it.

JESUITS RAISED CANE. Sugar cane first appeared as a crop in America in 1751. The Jesuits, who arrived in 1724 to build a mission, planted their first cane crop from Santo Domingo on their plantation that extended roughly from Our Lady of the Immaculate Conception Church (Jesuit Church on Baronne) to a point near Felicity Street, and from South Broad to the river. The Pontchartrain Expressway bisects it just about into two equal parts.

Cane grew there like grass from the beginning. At first its molasses was used simply as a sweetener. From it also came tafia, a beverage whose stupefying effects were popular in some quarters. Not until 1795 was Etienne de Bore successful in granulating sugar from the cane on his plantation in the area of Audubon Park. Like cotton, sugar made many Louisiana fortunes. The venerable Sugar Bowl football classic was born on the site of the old de Bore plantation.

'LADIES', *FILLES* & URSULINES. In addition to mosquitoes, swamps, rain, heat, fever and mud Bienville complained about the loneliness of his men. He wrote home bemoaning the fact that builders of the new colony were running wild in the woods "after Indian wenches." A sympathetic French monarch issued an order: "Collect all the women from the correction houses in Paris and ship them to *Nouvelle Orleans*." Eighty-eight of Paris' least esteemed females arrived in 1721 along with a trusty midwife whose pet name was La Sans-Regret. That's the way the story goes.

Bienville was sorely disappointed in the king's selection of mates for his men. Many of them were over 50, looked older, and in no condition to fetch much on the streets of Paris. However, most of Bienville's sailors were not particular. They married the women.

By no means were these Parisian street ladies the famous casket girls or *filles a la cassette,* sometimes taken for the former. The latter did not appear in New Orleans until 1728 seven years after the last shipload of erring ladies arrived.

The casket girls came as intended wives for a better class of colonists. New Orleans had its goodly share of idlers and drunkards, but quality people also came to make their fortunes in the new city. The young ladies were of peasant stock, many from orphanages, whom the Ursuline nuns agreed to shelter, feed and chaperone until a suitable proposal of marriage was offered.

Each girl arrived with a casket (a small basket) with her dowry from the king - four sheets, a blanket, two pairs of stockings, a hat, a pelisse - and wearing a smile.

Their first glimpse of the colony from their approaching boat startled the young women. It was crude, dirty and noisy. A swamp and woods were close by, where, they were warned, "hideous animals" roamed. However, the people seemed friendly and ladies wore fashionable gowns as they walked on *banquettes* (planks over mud) and hopped over open gutters.

Mother Superior met the girls at the gangplank and led them on the brief walk to the Ursulines' quarters owned by Bienville in the third block of Chartres. Along the way gentlemen tipped their hats. The nuns were kind and caring. And on guard.

Immediately the *filles a la cassette* were the talk of the

town. News of their arrival reached New England Puritans, many of whom thought that *filles a la cassette* were "ladies of the streets." Because the women were in such close contact with saintly nuns the Creoles accepted them as almost equals.

Quickly, with Mother Superior's nod, many of the girls were married and living happily ever after. Only one of the first shipment of casket girls embraced the habit, all others embraced suitable husbands. The king continued to send shiploads of such marital prospects to the city for the next 30 years or so.

The first handful of Ursulines arrived in 1727. They taught daughters of the colonists as well as others and nursed the ill. The nuns became a New Orleans institution and dynamic characters in the city's history. They still educate girls at their Uptown campus. It was they who pleaded unceasingly for heavenly intervention during the Battle of New Orleans where the mighty British were overcome by backwoodsmen in short order. The nuns have continuously encouraged devotion to Our Lady of Prompt Succor, patroness of New Orleans and Louisiana by papal decree. And also eternal friend of Gen. Andy Jackson.

IN THE NAME OF THE FATHER. Blessing oneself when passing a church was taught so zestfully by nuns in parochial schools that pupils were in high school before they were certain it wasn't sinful to pass a church without blessing oneself. To be safe many blessed themselves when passing protestant churches, synagogues, or other imposing structures such as the Jerusalem Temple. Children observed that women made the sign of the cross while bowing their heads, but men tipped their hats when passing a church. Why the difference was never explained.

A boy worried that blessing himself publicly might appear unmanly. He wore no hat to express reverence when passing a church. Adding to his dilemma were girls who made magnanimous outward signs of reverence with sweeping

145

motions of their arms, and closing their eyes. Some genuflected on sidewalks or in streetcar aisles. Meanwhile, their sexual counterparts made the barest gestures.

I knew a boy who dipped his head to the floor in streetcars before blessing himself, pretending to be retrieving a fallen book. The flashes of guilt were fleeting, I soon discovered.

Today, one may notice that all nun's do not bless themselves when passing a church, though the trick is not so much to spot the gesture but the nun. I know people who still bless themselves in public, but hurriedly.

DE RIGUER FOR CANAL ST. The single most recognizable change in New Orleans streets is the public dress code. It used to be that if you were on Canal Street you were dressed as best you could manage, whatever your age.

The three-piece suit, white shirt and tie, wing tip shoes and hat was de rigueur for the New Orleans businessman. A gentleman went no place without wearing a hat, except church. There he held it in his hand. He wore a felt hat in fall and winter and a Panama or straw katy in summer.

Women never entered a church without wearing a hat. Their mothers, grandmothers, great grandmothers and their mothers all had worn hats in church. Nobody asked why.

When on Canal Street ladies wore gloves. My mother had a "glove drawer" in her vanity dresser, a piece of boudoir furniture so named because its movable hinged mirrors offered views of one's coiffure and figure from all angles. When rushing to leave the house she would call out, "Has anybody been in my glove drawer?" My father and I accepted it as a rhetorical question.

If a woman could find only one glove of a pair that matched her particular ensemble it was permissible for her to carry the one glove. Having, not necessarily wearing, was the dictate.

A lady on Canal street was properly corsetted and coiffed, and with silk stocking seams straight and all accessories coordinated. Men were perfectly groomed also, but unobtrusively so. Had a man's attire attracted attention he would have hung his head, run home and changed.

Men were fashion clones long before the word was popular. They wore brown, black and navy blue, sometimes charcoal gray suits. Shirts were white. Only grandstanders wore colors that made them stand out. In summer seersucker or white linen suits were standard uniforms.

"SHINE, MISTAH?" The city's business section streets were rife with shoe shine parlors and sidewalk "shine" stands. Most barbershops had shiners on duty. On the way to an appointment a man could get a splendid spit-and-polish shine. Many were fresh-air businesses, right on the banquettes under awnings, and some with as many as three shiners who were always busy. They offered customers time to sit, relax, thumb through the newspaper and hear the radio.

EVERYBODY DELIVERED. Not so long ago there was no need for an Orleanian to travel any place for any necessity except a dental appointment. Physicians came to the house to paint throats, thump chests and search ears. Dry cleaners came to the house to pick up soiled and drop off cleaned clothing. Drugstores delivered, as did butchers - often by bicycle - and all department and clothing stores. Even ice was delivered. And cream cheese. And the service was free.

"Oh, Mr. Olivier," my mother would moan to the cleaner at the front door, "you didn't get that spot out."

"Aw. Shucks. OK. I'll be back with it before five."

'EVE-NIN MISS DE LA HOUSSAYE. Neighborhood children were instructed to greet adult neighbors when passing their houses. It was polite. "When you pass Mrs. de la Houssaye's house if she's sitting on the porch be sure you say, 'Good evening, Mrs. de la Houssaye.'" The average kid would have preferred his chances in the zoo's tiger cage. Many times I passed Mrs. de la Houssaye's house with eyes cast down, and mumbling swiftly and inaudibly in one breath,

"Eveninmissdelahoussaye."

On one occasion, I discovered that my mother was on our porch chatting with a neighbor, and she asked, "Did you greet Mrs. de la Houssaye when you passed?"

"Umm-uhh."

"I didn't hear you."

Sometimes being polite was embarassing. I often walked out of my way to reach home without passing Mrs. de la Houssaye's house.

TAMALE HOUSES. The ultimate treat in the early 30s were hot tamales made in the kitchens and sold in the front rooms of small houses in neighborhoods where streets were narrow and treeless, in the section called Marigny today. The only light source was a 30-watt bulb in a pull-chain socket in the parlor ceiling. The owners spoke a foreign language, smiled a lot and handed out the steaming hot tamales wrapped in butcher paper and rolled in newspaper. They were eaten mad hot in the car. Tamale houses depended on word-of-mouth advertising. When very young I was allowed to "have a taste" of one tamale. I well remember the first night I was given a whole tamale. My fingers and face were slippery with the orange grease on the steaming hot corn husk wrappings. And inside of me a fire raged from tongue to some point below my ribs. I have loved them since.

GRANDMA BEADS. Of the human condition's many strange manifestations "grandma beads" was among the most curious. A kid who came in from play without a pair of "grandma beads" on his neck was not enjoying himself to the fullest. "Grandma beads" appeared only in summertime when the sunshine was hot enough to kindle them. The beads were a combination of sweat and dirt that accumulated around and lodged in the creases of the neck. The ring of dirt arranged itself in strands of black balls, evenly spaced and perfectly shaped to appear as a necklace. The phenomenon was likened to jet beads commonly worn by ladies of grandmother vintage.

SWIM OR SINK? The most important thing one had to remember about going swimming was the time. The swimmer's first question asked was, "What time is it?" There was a rule, nay, a commandment that dictated exactly how long after dining one was to go swimming. It made no difference if the hopeful swimmer had eaten a whole cold chicken and minestrone soup or jelly on cracker, the waiting period was two hours. Once the food entered the mouth swimming automatically was postponed. Wise people waited 15 minutes longer. Wiser ones thought of doing something else. As kids we were never quite sure what happened to the incorrigible ones who might ignore the rule. It was too scary to contemplate.

After lunch in Covington we'd sit, barefooted and suited in the pavilion, a big wooden and odorous room open on three sides and set in a clump of trees a short distance from the beach. We'd watch the big round clock counting the time. Those were the only times when a Milky Way temptation was overpowered.

When drownings made the front pages of the newspaper, informed sources were often quoted as stating, "Ralph had just et a ershta poboy before he dove in. "

CRAWLING WITH AUNTS. For generations in New Orleans it was possible for kids to acquire many aunts and uncles, even though their parents might not have had siblings. It was common practice for kids to address their parents' very best friends as "aunt" or "uncle". The practice recognized a family's longtime friends as dearer than someone who would be called Mr. or Mrs. by their children. My parents' close friends became by parental decree my "aunt" or "uncle." And, in my youth a female friend of my mother might have become an "aunt" without the woman's mate necessarily earning the tag "uncle." Such a man would have been addressed by his given name preceded by the usual male title. He would become "Mr. John." So that couple would be "Aunt Sophie" and "Mr. John". Of course, their children were not recognized as cousins. There were instances when family friends were called neither "aunt" nor "uncle" by the children but "Mister Stan" and "Miss Kate."

"Mister Stan" and "Miss Kate" were warmer friends than "Mr. and Mrs. Hebert," for instance. The Hebert's might not have met the child until he was out of knickers. They could hardly have become an "aunt" or "uncle".

An adult's demeanor had a lot to do with how they were addressed by children. I recall that I had an "aunt" Dora but her husband was "Mr. Robichaux." Mr. Robichaux never smiled and appeared to be ready to leave wherever he was as soon as he arrived. He never lighted in one spot long enough to be called "uncle" or "Mr. Andre."

I am delighted that our grandchildren have some unrelated "aunts" and "uncles." Such winsome familiarity should not end with their generation.

VIVE LA DIFFERENCE. There was a time when a man could not have been found in a department store (unless he was a "floor walker" with a carnation in his lapel), nor a woman in a hardware store, unless she was delivering lunch to her husband, the proprietor. When Canal street was the shopping mecca in New Orleans men could be spotted on their way from the office to a barber shop or shoe shine parlor or restaurant. They were not going to D.H. Holmes, New Orleans esteemed department store now extinct, and called "Home-zez" by many.

In his entire lifetime my father never once ventured alone into a store to buy so much as a tie or pair of socks for himself. He never met a single soul "under the clock at Holmes"- the Orleanians' traditional meeting place. My mother selected suits for him that were delivered. If they fit he wore them. If not my mother returned them. He did not appear in person even to purchase shoes. She bought them and he wore them.

Today's malls are filled with men of a different shopping mentality. They search for a battery-operated nostril hair trimmer or red sweater. Actually, men do not shop but go to stores to purchase a particular item, perhaps a pair of socks when down to the last two of different color. Men who are not steady on their feet could be knocked over by the more aggressive female shoppers who sail through racks of merchandise with fortitude and glee. And there isn't a floor walker with boutonniere in his lapel in the entire town.

A man views shopping as having purpose. That's not at all how a woman sees it. For a female it's a lark, a way to pass time. There is no definite intent to purchase. They want to see what's available, to touch things, pick them up and hold them out to look at them. They even carry merchandise outside to see how "natural light" affects it. They may even try on a few things with no serious intent to purchase.

The woman shopper compares, sort of like teasing herself. The weak among them may actually purchase something she doesn't want. Solace comes with a sense of frugality in returning it. More disciplined types merely walk on, resisting the urge to buy until their feet ache. "Let's go, my feet hurt." That signals the conclusion of the shopping venture.

MIRACLE ON RUE DAUPHINE. A rather extraordinary event Downtown illustrates the Orleanians' deeply rooted, out-in-the-open spirituality. They burn votive candles like arsonists.

It occurred when the city was in the grip of one of its yellow fever scourges, the one of 1867. It seemed to gallop through town and was raging when Father Peter Leonard Thevis stepped off the boat from Cologne. His assignment was Holy Trinity Church, 3015 Dauphine Street (where my parents would be married 54 years later) in the old *Faubourg des Allemands* (suburb of the Germans), bordering the French's *Faubourg Marigny*.

As soon as the priest settled in the rectory he beseeched parishioners to pray to St. Roch for protection from the fever. From his pulpit he told of Europe's respect for the saint who was patron of the diseased, and who had survived the wrath of Black Plague in 14th century Tuscany. "St. Roch merely made the sign of the cross over those stricken and they were healed," the priest told them.

Old timers were astounded to hear of the miracle worker and rushed to church to burn candles. Even the Creoles, who numbered many saints among their heavenly acquaintances and had never heard of St. Roch, prayed.

As cholera joined the fever and the city braced for new crisis, the priest prayerfully sought St. Roch's intercession for the safety of his flock. If the people were spared Father Trevis promised to build a special chapel to honor the saint in a cemetery that would bear his name. From that moment, Father Thevis wrote in his record book, "Not one member of the Holy Trinity parish died of cholera or yellow fever."

Jacob Schoen, the undertaker who buried all parishioners, substantiated that claim. He announced that his business records revealed that not one funeral was recorded at the church during the siege.

At first the city refused to build *Campo Santa*(St. Roch) cemetery, but eventually approved the plan, and the cemetery was built. The tiny chapel was opened in 1875, with much of the labor having been done by the priest. His remains rest beneath the center aisle in the little Gothic structure that towers above rows of white tombs.

At the shrine are numerous stone tablets of thanksgiving (*merci*) alongside crutches and braces left through the years by those whose bodies were restored. Some claim that Father Thevis was responsible for the most remarkable happening in Downtown New Orleans. The priest gave all the credit to St. Roch.

THE ORIGINAL ORIGINAL. Vaguely, I recall the original Martin's restaurant, a major Downtown attraction, where the original Poor Boy sandwich was created. The place was big, bright and noisy and filled with the scent of food. We sat on stools at a counter where I was given a quarter loaf of French bread the pieces of which were parted by two inches of double-rowed plump fried oysters, crispy and hot. It was as long as my forearm. My parents would order several sandwiches, some oyster, some shrimp to take out. We carried two big brown bags filled with them. The bags were

warm and the toasty smell of their contents filled the car on the way to my grandparents' house. After all dined on the sandwiches that were warmed in the oven, the big round table was cleared and parents, siblings and their mates played poker.

Under cover of a fluffy quilt I'd fall asleep in a great tester bed after staring glassy-eyed at flames flickering in the fireplace's coal basket. The following morning - as though by magic - I'd awaken in my own bed at home. I had been wrapped in a blanket - "like a papoose" - placed on the rear seat of the car, removed from the the blanket and set gently into my bed. That's what they told me.

Poor Boys also came with roast beef and gravy (globs of it dripped on a boy's shirt) or combination ham and swiss- with lettuce and tomato but never on Fridays, days of abstinence from meat, and also family poker night.

Later, my mother's Uncle Herman Boesch designed a new building for Martin Brothers on St. Claude. I went there twice or so but was then too old to tag along with my parents as a "papoose." Delightfully fixed in my memory are those "original Poor Boys" and blazing coals on cold winter evenings at Grandma's.

GAWD, I LOVE NEW ORLEANS but not because it's perfect. In my estimation New Orleans' picks up minus points from those damnable hurricanes. Those scourges have been coming to where New Orleans is for centuries. Columbus and Bienville witnessed "great storms." These swept by the Louisiana coast before the Europeans came, even before the Indians, perhaps millenniums ago before living creatures.

Today we know all about such storms that originate over oceans in tropical regions near the equator, especially in the West Indian region, the Caribbean Sea and Gulf of Mexico. Their winds blow circularly around a low-pressure center called "eye of the storm." Ho-hum.

In her definitive and fascinating account of such storms in "Hurricane" Marjory Stoneman Douglas tells us that the Arawaks, an ancient people along the South American coast, came upon another ancient people who dwelt in caves. The Arawaks called them Rock Men because much of their time was spent carving on cave walls.

Some experts say the drawings depict fearful persons running from mighty evil forces - hurricanes. Others who study racial origins believe that before the Rock Men another group who witnessed hurricanes called them by name. Did their word, author Douglas suggests, passed down and combined with that of others, finally sound something like hurricane?

Words sounding like hurricane were used by some peoples to mean "evil spirit." Others used the word *yuracan, yurakon* and *yoroko*. The powerful Mayan god that controlled nature's forces was *jurakon*.

The first written account using the word hurricane are in notes of Bishop Landa, remembered through the ages as the man who burned the Mayan empire's documents.

In 1464 he wrote: " ... about six o'clock in the evening there arose a wind which kept increasing and soon changed into a hurricane of four winds."

Some speculate that perhaps somewhere lie the remains

of a man who took to his grave the secret of how the English word hurricane came about. Was it on that fateful day when a man, huffing and puffing with howling winds lapping at his posterior, ran as his terrified wife, Mary Cane, yelled: "Hurry, Cane!?"

New Orleanians weren't utterly fascinated with hurricanes until television and its meterologists came into their houses with live pictures of awesome destruction that was "moving up the coast a piece."

It used to be, in our old neighborhood, that after a storm we awakened, observed the turmoil outside and commented, "Umpph. That was some storm last night."

Nowadays Orleanians stay up all night clutching batteries, candles and canned soups watching TV, cringing and speculating. "My God! 180 miles an hour and 25-foot tides. I told you. I begged you to get more sandbags. Did you pay the flood insurance?"

Some have developed into hurricane zealots, marking storm tracing maps and checking kerosene lamps. "This one is comin' right at us, just like that killer one. Let's go up in the attic and check the air in our rafts. Boy, oh-boy, are we lucky I bought them life preservers. And canoe."

It's to a point now that in hurricane season sitcoms and dramas get second billing to meteorologists. The fact is we know too much about hurricanes. New Orleans was perfect when we were dumber.

PICK A WHAT? The first newspaper in New Orleans was *Le Moniteur de la Louisiane*. The oldest issue on record is No. 26 dated August 21, 1796. When it began publication is uncertain, and it ceased long ago. Through the centuries newspapers printed in several languages have come and gone in New Orleans, but the most enduring is the one with the engaging name. *The Times-Picayune* was born in 1914 with the merging of *The Picayune,* founded in 1837 and *The Times-Democrat*, a creature of an 1881 merger of *The Times*, founded in 1863 and *The Democrat*, founded in 1875.

The Picayune was established by George Wilkins Kendall and F.A. Lumsden, some said as a hobby more than because of great demand. The Picayune's name (affectionately known in its heyday as The Pic) has fascinated generations of readers. A picayune was a small silver coin valued at 6 1/4

cents, the cost of an issue of the paper. When it first appeared on January 25, 1837, in a one paragraph editorial the newspaper's owners stated: "This day we present the public with the first number of The Picayune ... we do not boast the capacity in size or sense of our contemporaries. We profess we do a small business and being only a picayune concern. It remains for the public at large to make much of us. At No. 36 Gravier Street ... our paper may be had with good endorsers for six and one-quarter per cent every day, Sunday included."

Whatever it took the partners did to make "The Pic" something better than others. It was launched into national prominence when it was 10 years old. Then Kendall straddled a mule on the West Bank and plodded along to the Mexican War. He traveled day and night, stopping only to arrange delivery of his news reports from one point to another until they would reach New Orleans. The newspaperman wrote eyewitness accounts of war directly from the battlefield. Even Washington readers were impressed. The whole country was talking about George Wilkins Kendall, the first American war correspondent, and "The Picayune's pony express."

In 1860 Kendall's friend Lumsden and all his family drowned in the Great Lakes when the steamer Lady Elgin sank. Kendall traveled extensively in Europe, always sending home special messages to New Orleans. He died in 1867.

After Lumsden's death, Alva M. Holbrook bought an interest in the paper that continued to be a prominent American journal through the Civil War. When federal troops occupied the city the newspaper was suppressed by order of the commanding general, and though allowed to publish again two months later, it remained at odds with occupation forces until they departed.

After the death of Holbrook in 1867, his widow Mrs. Alva Morris Holbrook (Eliza Jane Poitevent), became the newspaper's sole owner and publisher. At the time she was 27 and the only female owner of a large daily newspaper in the world. However, the paper was in debt $80,000.

Refusing to walk away from what many considered an awesome task, she called together her staff and announced: "I am a woman. Some of you may not want to work for a woman. If so you may leave now with full recommendations, and no hard feelings. But those of you who remain, will you give me your undivided loyalty?" The staffers who cheered her statement were long acquainted with her. She was the popular poet from rural Mississippi whose work appeared in *The Picayune* under the by-line Pearl Rivers.

Among her supporters was the paper's business manager George Nicholson. Not only did he have confidence in her ability but he backed her with his savings. He also married her.

Immediately she introduced innovations and brightened the paper with human interest features that were sometimes sassy.

She also introduced her friend Elizabeth Gilmore who was to become an internationally famed writer known as Dorothy Dix. She gave advice to lovesick readers of 200 papers on three continents, and was the highest paid woman in her field. Her career extended into the Great Depression era under *The Times-Picayune* banner.

Those pioneers and innovators were just a few among many distinguished publishers, managers, editors and writers at the 159-year-old New Orleans' institution still known by many as "*The Picayune.*"

AND LEFT, IF YOU WANT. The single most aggravation in New Orleans history is not hurricanes, not even the yellow fever epidemics. Not even the Grand Prix du Mardi Gras with its racing cars screeching through the central busines district. Hands down it is the law that invites Orleanians to TURN RIGHT ON RED.

Resident drivers and those suburbanites who drive in and out, consider the convenience a license to TURN LEFT, IF YOU WANT. You'll see drivers turn left on red. Worse, you'll see drivers TURN RIGHT ON RED directly in the path of oncoming cars.

For generations motorists in New Orleans have been known to zip straight ahead on red. It doesn't matter that other cars are coming. Here are remarks from a recent interview with a former New Orleans driver who moved to the suburbs "where it's safer."

"Sir, we are told that you moved to the suburbs because it's safer."

"Yeah, it's da troot."

"But we just saw you run a red light."

"Nobody was comin'. It was safe. Dij-ja notice how I zoomed up to 50, just in case?"

"But it is against the law to run a red light."

"I owny do dat when no cars are comin'."

"Sir, a car was coming. My car."

"And how fas was you goin'?"

"I was going exactly 30 miles an hour."

"Well, then, ya see dere? I was goin' 48. You could-da never hit me. I was safe."

"Tell me, sir, what do the red, yellow and green lights indicate?"

"The Red, that there means to stop when a car is crossin'

in front-a ya. Yellow means hurry up 'cause Red is next. And Green means to go on ahead no matta wut 'cause you got the right-a way."

"You are incorrigible."

"No I ain't. I got insurance."

C'EST DIFFERENT, C'EST TOUT

Unique is a tiresome word, and unreliable. But the word best describes New Orleans. The town's uniqueness is reflected not only in its appearance and design but also in the ways of its people. The place and the people give the old girl a spirit that tickles visitors and residents alike.

This spirit is easier experienced than described. The visitor immediately senses this special something. The native doesn't define it.

From the day Bienville arrived with his colonial cadre, the settlement that was skirted by water on all sides was destined to be different.

The colony flourished into a city whose inhabitants were French, Spanish, native Indian, African, Caribbean, German, English, Irish and Italian and some others. They spoke at least nine languages while adapting their tongues to the

American sound. The people were white, black and red. And *cafe au lait* colored. Political authority changed hands six times. Manners and customs ran the gamut. A kind of music was born. So was a cuisine. Priestly blessings were as numerous as sorcerers' spells. There was promise of naughty adventure behind the Quarter's shuttered windows along the *banquettes*, balanced with reverence in pews and repentence in dark confessionals. Today they still whoop it up in the old Quarter's ancient streets. Even today flood waters rush into houses and the stubborn occupants sweep it out along with the carpet.

Old New Orleans experienced physical changes, but with altered landscape and lifestyles the townspeople continue to relish and respect ways of the past. By clinging to their traits they make their city uncommon, a singular experience.

Hurry, here comes the parade! This is no ordinary place. It's different, it's everything.

God gave us our memories so that we may have roses in December

James Barrie (1860-1937), Scotish novelist